LOWER & ON-LEVEL MENUS
GRADES 6–8

Differentiating Instruction With Menus for the Inclusive Classroom

Language Arts

LOWER & ON-LEVEL MENUS
GRADES 6–8

Differentiating Instruction With Menus for the Inclusive Classroom

Language Arts

Laurie E. Westphal

Routledge
Taylor & Francis Group
NEW YORK AND LONDON

First published in 2013 by Prufrock Press Inc.

Published in 2021 by Routledge
605 Third Avenue, New York, NY 10017
2 Park Square, Milton Park, Abingdon, Oxon OX14 4RN

Routledge is an imprint of the Taylor & Francis Group, an informa business.

Production Design by Raquel Trevino

Library of Congress Cataloging-in-Publication Data

Westphal, Laurie E., 1967-
Differentiating instruction with menus for the inclusive classroom. Language arts, grades 6-8 / by Laurie E. Westphal.
pages cm
Includes bibliographical references.
ISBN 978-1-59363-963-1 (pbk.)
1. Language arts (Elementary) 2. Language arts (Middle school) 3. Individualized instruction. 4. Inclusive education. 5. Mixed ability grouping in education. I. Title.
LB1576.W4847 2013
372.6--dc23

2012027451

ISBN-13: 978-1-0321-4295-1 (hbk)
ISBN-13: 978-1-5936-3963-1 (pbk)

DOI: 10.4324/9781003234227

CONTENTS

Author's Note

If you are familiar with books on various differentiation strategies, then you probably know about my Differentiating Instruction With Menus series, and you may be wondering about the differences between that series and this one, the Differentiating Instruction With Menus for the Inclusive Classroom series. In fact, when we first discussed creating this series, my editor asked how we could avoid having one series "cannibalize" (graphic, but a great word!) the other. Well, here is how I envision the two series being used:

These two series stand on their own if:

- You teach mostly lower ability, on-level, and ESL students and would like to modify your lessons on your own to accommodate a few advanced students. In this case, use this series, Differentiating Instruction With Menus for the Inclusive Classroom.
- You teach mostly advanced and high-ability students and would like to modify your lessons on your own to accommodate a few lower level students. In this case, use the Differentiating Instruction With Menus series.

These two series can serve as companions to one another if:

- You teach students with a wide range of abilities (from special education to gifted) and would benefit from having a total of three menus for a given topic of study: those for lower ability and on-level students (provided by this series, Differentiating Instruction With Menus for the Inclusive Classroom) and those for high-ability students (provided by the Differentiating Instruction With Menus series).

The menu designs used in this book reflect a successful modification technique I began using in my own classroom as the range of my students' ability levels widened. I experimented with many ways to use menus, from having students of all ability levels using the same menu with the same expectations, to having everyone using the same menu with modified contracted expectations, to using leveled menus where each student received one of three menus with some overlapping activities based on readiness, abilities, or preassessment results. I found that if the students in a given classroom had similar ability levels, I could use one menu with every student with slight modifications; however, the greater the span of ability levels, the more I needed the different leveled menus to reach everyone. Each book in the Differentiating Instruction With Menus for the Inclusive Classroom series has two leveled menus for the objectives covered: a lower level menu indicated by a ▲ and an on-level menu indicated by a ●. This way, teachers can provide more options to students with diverse abilities in the inclusive classroom. If used with the corresponding book in the Differentiating Instruction With Menus series, the teacher has a total of three leveled menus to work with.

Many teachers have told me how helpful the original Differentiating Instruction With Menus books are and how they have modified the books' menus to meet the needs of their lower level students. Teachers are always the first to make adjustments and find solutions, but wouldn't it be great if they had these preparations and changes already made for them? This is the purpose of the Differentiating Instruction With Menus for the Inclusive Classroom series.

—Laurie E. Westphal

Chapter 1

Choice in the Inclusive Middle School Classroom

> "When it comes to my sixth-grade math classroom, who *isn't* my audience?"
>
> *—Sixth-grade teacher, when asked to describe her target audience during a menu-writing session*

Let's begin by addressing the concept of the inclusive classroom. The term inclusive (vs. exclusive) leads one to believe that we are discussing a situation in which all students are included. In the simplest of terms, that is exactly what we are referring to as an inclusive classroom: a classroom that may have special needs students, on-level students, bilingual or ESL students, and gifted students. Although the concept is a simple one, the considerations are significant.

When thinking about the inclusive classroom and its unique ambiance, one must first consider the needs of the range of students within the classroom. Mercer, Lane, Jordan, Allsopp, and Eisele (1996) stated it best in their assessment of the needs in an inclusive classroom:

DOI: 10.4324/9781003234227-1

> Students who are academically gifted, those who have had abundant experiences, and those who have demonstrated proficiency with lesson content typically tend to perform well when instruction is anchored at the "implicit" end of the instructional continuum. In contrast, low-performing students (i.e., students at risk for school failure, students with learning disabilities, and students with other special needs) and students with limited experience or proficiency with lesson content are most successful when instruction is explicit. Students with average academic performance tend to benefit most from the use of a variety of instructional methods that address individual needs. Instructional decisions for most students, therefore, should be based on assessment of individual needs. (pp. 230–231)

Acknowledging these varied and often contradictory needs that arise within an inclusive classroom can lead to frustration when trying to make one assignment or task fit everyone's needs. There are few—if any—traditional, teacher-directed lessons that can be implicit, explicit, and based on individual needs all at the same time. There is, however, one technique that tries to accomplish this: choice.

Choice: The Superman of Techniques in the Inclusive Middle School Classroom?

> "I like being able to choose. I can pick what I am good at!"
>
> *–Eighth-grade social studies student*

Can the offering of appropriate choices really be the hero of the inclusive middle school classroom? Can it leap buildings in a single bound and meet the needs of our implicit, explicit, and individual interests? Yes. By considering the use and benefits of choice, we can see that by offering choices, teachers really can meet the needs of the whole range of students in an inclusive classroom. Ask adults whether they would prefer to choose what to do or be told what to do, and of course, they will say they would prefer to have a choice. Students have the same feelings. Although they may not be experienced in making choices, they will make choices based on their needs, just as adults do—which makes everyone involved in the inclusive experience a little less stressed and frustrated.

Why Is Choice Essential to Middle School Students?

> "Almost every kid my age wants to be able to choose what they want to work on. They just do."
>
> *—Eighth-grade math student, when asked if he thought choice was important in his classes*

When considering the appropriateness of choice for middle school students, no matter their ability level, we begin by considering who (or what) our middle school students personify. During their years in middle school, adolescents struggle to determine who they are and how they fit into the world around them. They constantly try new ideas (that peroxide in the hair sounded like a good idea at the time!), new experiences (if you sit on the second-floor roof of your home one more time, I will tell your parents!), and a constant flux of personalities (preppy one day, dark nails and lipstick the next) in order to find themselves. During this process, which can take anywhere from a few months to a few years, depending on the child, children don't always have academics at the forefront of their minds. Thus, instruction and products have to engage the individuals whom these students are trying to become.

The Benefits of Choice

> "I am different in the way I do stuff. I like to build stuff with my hands."
>
> *—Sixth-grade student, when asked why he enjoyed activities that allow choice*

One benefit of choice is a greater sense of independence for the students, including some who have not had the opportunity to think about their own learning in the past. What a powerful feeling! Students will be designing and creating products based on what they envision, rather than what their teacher envisions. There is a possibility for more than one "right" product; all students can make products their own, no matter their level of ability. When students would enter my middle school classroom, they had often been trained by previous teachers to produce exactly what the teacher wanted, not what the students thought would be best. Teaching my students that what they envisioned could be correct (and wonderful) was often a struggle. "Is this what you want?" and "Is this right?" were popular questions as we started the school year. Allowing students to have choices in the products they create to demonstrate their learning helps create independence at any age, within any ability level.

> "[Choice] puts me in a good mood to participate!"
>
> *—Seventh-grade student*

Middle school students already have started transitioning from an academic focus to more of a social one. Choice is a way to help bring their focus back to the more desired (at least from everyone else's point of view) academic aspect of school. When students have choices in the activities they wish to complete, they are more focused on the learning that leads to their chosen products. Students become excited when they learn information that can help them develop a product they would like to create. Students pay close attention to instruction and have an immediate application for the knowledge being presented in class. Also, if students are focused, they are less likely to be off task during instruction.

The final benefit (although I am sure there are many more) is the simple fact that by offering varied choices at appropriate levels, you can address implicit instructional options, explicit instructional options, and individual needs without anyone getting overly frustrated or overworked. Many a great educator has referred to the idea that the best learning takes place when the students have a desire to learn and can feel successful while doing it. Some middle school students still have a desire to learn anything that is new to them, but many others do not want to learn anything unless it is of interest to them. By choosing from different activities according to their interests and readiness, students stretch beyond what they already know, and by offering such choices, teachers create a void that needs to be filled. This void leads to a desire to learn.

A Point to Ponder: Making Good Choices Is a Skill

> "It's a good point. How can we expect children to make good choices when they haven't had the chance to make any yet?"
>
> *– Eighth-grade teacher, after hearing me discuss choice as a skill*

When we think of making a good choice as a skill, much like writing an effective paragraph, it becomes easy enough to understand the processes needed to encourage students to make their own choices. In keeping with this analogy, students could certainly figure out how to write on their own, and perhaps even how to compose sentences and paragraphs, by modeling other examples. Imagine, however, the progress and strength of the writing produced when students are given guidance and even the most basic of instructions on how to accomplish the task. The written piece is still their own, but the quality of the finished piece is much stronger when guidance is given during the process. The same is true with the quality of choices students can make in the classroom.

As with writing, students—especially those with special needs—could make choices on their own, but when the teacher provides background knowledge and assistance, the choices become more meaningful and the products richer. Although all students certainly need guidance, on-level and special needs students often will need the most guidance; they have usually not been in an educational setting that has allowed them to experience different products, and the idea of choice can be new to them. Some students may have experienced only basic instructional choices, like choosing between two journal prompts or perhaps having the option of making either a poster or a PowerPoint presentation about the content being studied. Some may not have experienced even this level of choice. This lack of experience may cause frustration for both teacher and student.

Teaching Choices as a Skill

So, what is the best way to provide guidance and enable middle school students to develop the skill of making good choices? First, identify the appropriate number of choices for your students. Although the goal might be to have students choose from 20 different options, teachers might start by having their students select from a smaller number of predetermined choices the first day (if they were using a Game Show menu, for instance, students might choose one activity from the first column). Then, after that product had been created, students could choose from another set of options a few days later, and perhaps from another set the following week. By breaking students' choices down, teachers reinforce how to approach or attack a more complex and/or varied choice format in the future. All students can work up to making complex choices from longer lists of options as their choice skill level increases.

Second, although our middle school students feel they know everything, they may still need guidance on how to select the option that is right for them (and not select something just because their friends select it!). They may not automatically gravitate toward options without an exciting and detailed description of each choice. For the most part, students have been trained to produce what the teacher requests, which means that when given a choice, they will usually choose what seems to be the easiest and what the teacher most wants (then they can get to what they would prefer to be doing). This means that when the teacher discusses the different menu options, he or she has to be equally as excited about each option. The discussion of the different choices has to be animated and specific. For example, if the content is all very similar, the focus should be on the product: "If you want to do some singing, then this one is for you!" or "If you want to write and draw, then check this one as a maybe!" Sometimes, options may differ based on both content and product, in which case both can be pointed out to students to assist them in making good choices for themselves. "You have some different choices in our ecosystems unit. If you want to do something with animals and the computer, then check this one as a maybe. If you are thinking you want to do something with specimen collecting and making an exhibit, then this one might be for you." The more exposure students have to the processing the teacher provides, the more skilled they become at making good choices.

How Can Teachers Provide Choices?

> "I was concerned at first that my students would be confused by so many options and that their focus and behavior might be impacted. Instead, they really responded well—I am going to encourage other teachers to use menus for choice."
>
> *—Middle school inclusion teacher, when asked how her students with special needs responded to having choices*

When people go to a restaurant, the common goal is to find something on the menu to satisfy their hunger. Students come into our classrooms having a hunger, as well—a hunger for learning. Choice menus are a way of allowing our students to choose how they would like to satisfy that hunger. At the very least, a menu is a list of choices that students use to choose an activity (or activities) they would like to complete to show what they have learned. At best, it is a complex system in which students earn points by making choices from different areas of study. All menus should also incorporate a free-choice option for those "picky eaters" who would like to make a special order to satisfy their learning hunger.

The next few sections provide examples of the main types of menus that will be used in this book. Each menu has its own benefits, limitations or drawbacks, and time considerations. An explanation of the free-choice option and its management will follow the information on each type of menu.

Meal Menu

> "My students appreciate and need choices. At first, they may need fewer at a time."
>
> *—Middle school inclusion teacher, when asked about her students with special needs having choices*

Description

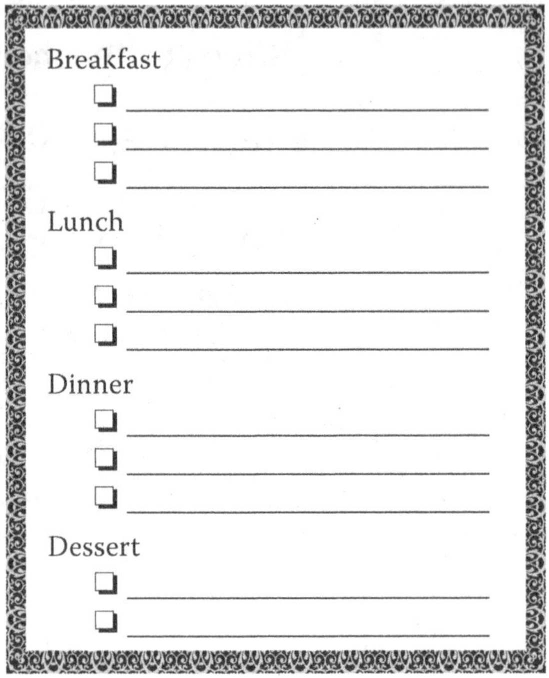

Figure 1.1. Meal menu.

The Meal menu (see Figure 1.1) is a menu with a total of at least nine predetermined choices as well as two or more enrichment options for students. The choices are created at the various levels of Bloom's Revised taxonomy (Anderson & Krathwohl, 2001) and incorporate different learning styles, with the levels getting progressively higher as students move from breakfast to lunch and then on to dinner. All products carry the same weight for grading and have similar expectations for completion time and effort. The enrichment (dessert) options can be used for extra credit or can replace another meal option at the teacher's discretion.

Benefits

User friendliness. This menu is very straightforward and easy to understand for students with special needs.

Flexibility. This menu can cover either one topic in depth or three different objectives, with each meal representing a different objective. With this menu, students have the option of completing three products: one from each meal.

Optional enrichment. Although the dessert category is not required, this part of the Meal menu allows students to have the option of going further or deeper if time permits.

Easily broken down. The Meal menu is very easy to break apart into smaller pieces for students who need support in making choices. Students could be asked to select a breakfast option while the rest of the menu is put on hold; then, once the breakfast product is submitted, they could select a lunch option, and so on.

Friendly design. Students quickly understand how to use this menu because of its real-world application.

Weighting. All products are equally weighted, so recording grades and maintaining paperwork are easily accomplished with this menu.

Short time period. This menu is intended for shorter periods of time, between 1–3 weeks.

Limitations

Few topics. This menu only covers one or three topics.

Time Considerations

This menu is usually intended for shorter periods of completion time—at most, it should take 3 weeks. If the menu focuses on one topic in depth, then it can be completed in one week.

Tic-Tac-Toe Menu

> "[Tic-Tac-Toe menus] can be a real pain. A lot of times I only liked two of the choices and had to do the last one. Usually I got stuck with a play or a presentation."
>
> *—Sixth-grade math student, when asked to step out of her comfort zone based on the tic-tac-toe design*

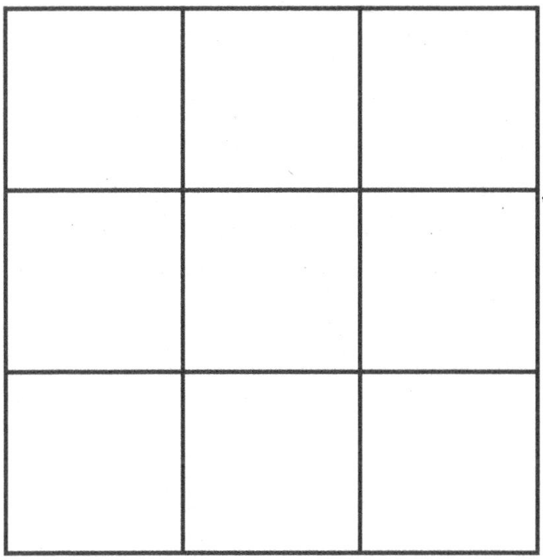

Figure 1.2. Tic-Tac-Toe menu.

Description

The Tic-Tac-Toe menu (see Figure 1.2) is a well-known, commonly used menu that contains a total of eight predetermined choices and, if appropriate, one free choice for students. Choices can be created at the same level of Bloom's Revised taxonomy or can be arranged in such a way to allow for three different levels or content areas. If all choices have been created at the same level of

Bloom's Revised taxonomy, then each choice has similar expectations for completion time and effort.

Benefits

Flexibility. This menu can cover either one topic in depth or three different topics, objectives, or even content areas. When this menu covers just one objective and all tasks are from the same level of Bloom's Revised taxonomy, students have the option of completing three projects in a tic-tac-toe pattern, or simply picking three from the menu. When the menu covers three objectives or different levels of Bloom's Revised taxonomy, students will need to complete a tic-tac-toe pattern (either a vertical column or horizontal row) to be sure they have completed one activity from each objective or level.

Stretching. When students make choices on this menu, completing a row or column based on its design, they will usually face one choice that is out of their comfort zone, be it for its level of Bloom's Revised taxonomy level, its product learning style, or its content. They will complete this "uncomfortable" choice because they want to do the other two in that row or column.

Friendly design. Students quickly understand how to use this menu. It is nonthreatening because it does not contain points, and therefore it seems to encourage students to stretch out of their comfort zones.

Weighting. All projects are equally weighted, so recording grades and maintaining paperwork is easily accomplished with this menu.

Short time period. This menu is intended for shorter periods of time, between 1–3 weeks.

Limitations

Few topics. This menu only covers one or three topics.

Student compromise. Although this menu does allow choice, a student will sometimes have to compromise and complete an activity he or she would not have chosen because it completes the required tic-tac-toe. (This is not always bad, though!)

Time Considerations

This menu is usually intended for shorter amounts of completion time—at the most, it should take 3 weeks with one product submitted each week. If the menu focuses on one topic in depth, it can be completed in one week.

List Menu

> "I like that you can add up the points to be more than 100, so even if you make some small mistakes, your grade could still be a 100."
>
> *–Seventh-grade student*

Figure 1.3. List menu.

Description

The List menu (see Figure 1.3), or Challenge List, is a more complex menu than the Tic-Tac-Toe menu, with a total of at least 10 predetermined choices, each with its own point value, and at least one free choice for students. Choices are simply listed with assigned points based on the levels of Bloom's Revised taxonomy. The choices carry different weights and have different expectations for completion time and effort. A point criterion is set forth that equals 100%, and students choose how they wish to attain that point goal.

Benefits

Responsibility. Students have complete control over their grades. They really like the idea that they can guarantee their grades if they complete the required work. If they lose points on one of the chosen assignments, then they can complete another to be sure they have met their goal points. This responsibility over their own grades also allows a shift in thinking about grades: whereas many students think of grades in terms of how the teacher judged their work, having control over their grades leads students to understand that they earn them.

Different learning levels. This menu also has the flexibility to allow for individualized contracts for different learning levels within the classroom. Each student can choose what products will provide the points for his or her 100%.

Concept reinforcement. This menu allows for an in-depth study of material; however, with the different levels of Bloom's Revised taxonomy being represented, students who are still learning the concepts can choose some of the lower level point value projects to reinforce the basics before jumping into the higher level activities.

Variety. A List menu offers a larger variety of product choices. There is guaranteed to be a product of interest to everyone.

Limitations

One topic. This menu is best used for one topic in depth, so that students don't miss any specific content.

Cannot guarantee objectives. If this menu is used for more than one topic, it is possible for a student to not complete an activity for each objective, depending on the choices he or she makes.

Preparation. Teachers need to have all materials ready at the beginning of the unit for students to be able to choose any of the activities on the list, which requires advanced planning. (Note: Once the materials are assembled, the menu is wonderfully low stress!)

Time Considerations

This menu is usually intended for shorter amounts of completion time—at the most, 2 weeks.

20-50-80 Menu

> "My least favorite menu is 20-50-80. You can't just do the easy ones. If you pick a 20, then you have to do an 80. No matter what, you have to do one of the hard ones."
>
> *—Seventh-grade student*

Description

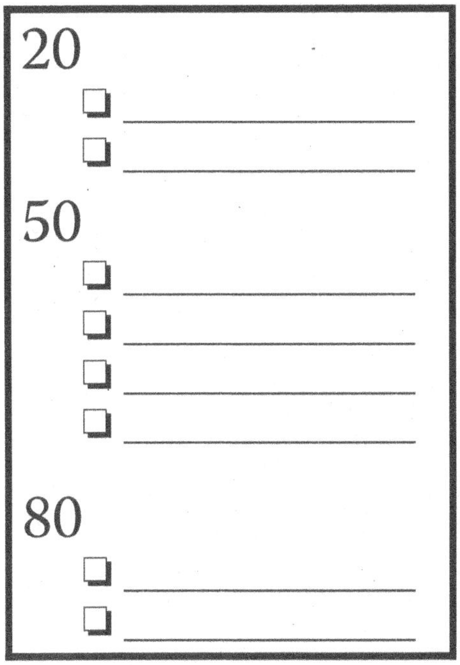

Figure 1.4. 20-50-80 menu.

A 20-50-80 menu (see Figure 1.4; also called a 2-5-8 menu, see Magner, 2000) is a variation on a List menu, with a total of at least eight predetermined choices: two choices with a point value of 20, at least four choices with a point value of 50, and at least two choices with a point value of 80. Choices are assigned points based on the levels of Bloom's Revised taxonomy. Choices with a point value of 20 represent the "remember" and "understand" levels, choices with a point value of 50 represent the "apply" and "analyze" levels, and choices with a point value of 80 represent the "evaluate" and "create" levels. All levels of choices carry different weights and have different expectations for completion time and effort. Students are expected to earn 100 points for a 100%. Students choose what combination they would like to use to attain that point goal.

Benefits

Responsibility. With this menu, students still have complete control over their grades.

Guaranteed activity. This menu's design is also set up in such a way that students must complete at least one activity at a higher level of Bloom's Revised taxonomy in order to reach their point goal.

Great introductory menu. This menu is one of the shortest menus; if students choose well, they can accomplish their goal by completing only two products. This menu is usually less daunting than some of the longer, more complex menus. It provides students a great introduction to the process of making choices.

Limitations

One topic. Although it can be used for more than one topic, this menu works best with an in-depth study of one topic.

Higher level thinking. Students may choose to complete only one activity at a higher level of thinking.

Time Considerations

This menu is usually intended for a shorter amount of completion time—at the most, one week.

Baseball Menu

> "There were so many choices, and most of them were fun activities!"
>
> *–Sixth-grade student*

Description

The Baseball menu (see Figure 1.5) is a baseball-based variation of the List menu with a total of at least 20 predetermined choices: choices are given values as singles, doubles, triples, or home runs based on the levels of Bloom's Revised taxonomy. Singles represent the remember and understand levels; doubles, the apply and analyze levels; triples, the evaluate level; and home runs, the create level. All levels of choices carry different weights and have different expectations for completion time and effort. Students are expected to earn a certain number of runs (around all four bases) for a 100%. Students choose what combination they would like to use to attain that number of runs.

Figure 1.5. Baseball menu.

Benefits

Responsibility. With this menu, students still have complete control over their own grades.

Flexibility and variety. This menu allows for many choices at each level. Students should have no trouble finding something that catches their interest.

Theme. This menu has a fun theme that students enjoy and can be used throughout the classroom. A bulletin board can be set up with a baseball diamond, with each student having his or her own player who can move through the bases. Not only can students keep track of their own RBIs, but they can also have a visual reminder of what they have completed.

Limitations

One topic. This menu is best used for one all-encompassing unit with many objectives for in-depth study.

Preparation. With so many choices available to students, teachers should have all materials ready at the beginning of the unit for students to be able to choose any of the activities on the list. This sometimes causes a consideration for space in the classroom.

Time Considerations

This menu is usually intended for a longer amount of completion time, depending on the number of runs required for a 100%—at the most, 4 or 5 weeks.

Game Show Menu

> "This menu was very easy to break down for my [students needing modifications], as we could focus on just one column at a time. They were very successful with the format."
>
> *—Seventh-grade science teacher*

Description

The Game Show menu (see Figure 1.6) is a complex menu. It covers multiple topics or objectives with at least three predetermined choices and a free-choice option for each objective. Choices are assigned points based on the levels of Bloom's Revised taxonomy. All choices carry different weights and have different expectations for completion time and effort. A point criterion is set forth that equals 100%. Students must complete at least one activity from each objective in order to reach their goal.

Figure 1.6. Game Show menu.

Benefits

Free choice. This menu allows many choices for students, but if they do not want to complete the offered activities, they can propose their own activity for each objective.

Responsibility. This menu allows students to guarantee their own grades.

Different learning levels. This menu has the flexibility to allow for individualized contracts for different learning levels within the classroom. Each student can contract for a certain number of points for his or her 100%.

Objectives guaranteed. The teacher is guaranteed that the students complete an activity from each objective covered, even if it is at a lower level.

Limitations

Confirm expectations. The only real limitation for this menu is that students (and parents) must understand the guidelines for completing the menu.

Time Considerations

This menu is usually intended for a longer amount of completion time. Although it can be used as a yearlong menu (each column could be for one grading period), it is usually intended for 2–3 weeks.

Free Choice in the Inclusive Classroom

> "I didn't do one [free choice] on the menu. I didn't really get it, but I saw a poster [as a free choice] that my friend did that was really cool. I think I want to do a free choice on the next one."
>
> *—Seventh-grade inclusion student*

Most of the menus included in this book allow students to submit a free-choice product. This is a product of their choosing that addresses the content being studied and shows what the student has learned about the topic. Although this option is available, students may not fully understand its benefits or immediately respond to the opportunity even after it has been explained. In the past, certain students may have been offered choices and enjoyed the idea of taking charge of their own learning; however, students with special needs may not have had much exposure to this concept. Their educational experiences tend to be objective-based and teacher-driven. This is not to say that they would not respond well to the idea of free choice; in fact, they can embrace it as enthusiastically as gifted students can. The most significant difference between these two groups successfully approaching free choice is the amount of content needed by the student before he or she embarks on a proposed option. Students with special needs need to feel confident in their knowledge of the content and information before they are ready to step out on their own, propose their own ideas, and create their own products. Gifted students may be comfortable with less knowledge and structure.

With most of the menus, the students are allowed to submit a free-choice product for their teacher's consideration. Figure 1.7 shows two sample proposal forms that have been used successfully in my classroom. With middle school students, this cuts down greatly on the whining that often accompanies any task given to students. A copy of these forms should be given to each student when the menu is first introduced. The form used is based on the type of menu being presented. For example, if you are using the Tic-Tac-Toe menu, there is no need to submit a point proposal. A discussion should be held with the students so they understand the expectations of a free choice. I always had a few students who

Name: ______________________________ Teacher's Approval: ______________

Free-Choice Proposal Form for Point-Based Menu

Points Requested: _____________ Points Approved: __________

Proposal Outline

1. What specific topic or idea will you learn about?

2. What criteria should be used to grade it? (Neatness, content, creativity, artistic value, etc.)

3. What will your product look like?

4. What materials will you need from the teacher to create this product?

Name: ______________________________ Teacher's Approval: ______________

Free-Choice Proposal Form

Proposal Outline

1. What specific topic or idea will you learn about?

2. What criteria should be used to grade it? (Neatness, content, creativity, artistic value, etc.)

3. What will your product look like?

4. What materials will you need from the teacher to create this product?

Figure 1.7. Sample proposal forms for free choice.

did not want to complete a task on the menu; students are welcome to create their own free-choice proposals and submit them for approval. The biggest complainers will not always go to the trouble to complete the form and have it approved, but it is their choice not to do so. The more free choice is used and encouraged, the more students will begin to request it. How the students show their knowledge will begin to shift from teacher-focused to student-designed activities. If students do not want to make a proposal using the proposal form after the teacher has discussed the entire menu and its activities, then they can place the unused form in a designated place in the classroom. Others may want to use their forms, and it is often surprising who wants to submit a proposal form after hearing about the opportunity!

Proposal forms must be submitted before students begin working on their free-choice products. The teacher then knows what the students are working on, and the student knows the expectations the teacher has for that product. Once the project has been approved, the form can easily be stapled to the student's menu sheet. The student can refer to the form while developing the free-choice product, and when the grading takes place, the teacher can refer to the agreement for the graded features of the product.

Each part of the proposal form is important and needs to be discussed with students:

- *Name/Teacher's Approval.* The student must submit this form to the teacher for approval. The teacher will carefully review all of the information, discuss any suggestions or alterations with the student, if needed, and then sign the top.
- *Points Requested.* Found only on the point-based menu proposal form, this is where negotiation may need to take place. Students usually will submit their first request for a very high number (even the 100% goal). They tend to equate the amount of time something will take with the number of points it should earn. But please note that the points are always based on the levels of Bloom's Revised taxonomy. For example, a PowerPoint presentation with a vocabulary word quiz would get minimal points, although it may have taken a long time to create. If the students have not been exposed to the levels of Bloom's Revised taxonomy, this can be difficult to explain. You can always refer to the popular "Bloom's Verbs" to help explain the difference between time-consuming and higher level activities.

- *Points Approved.* Found only on the point-based menu proposal form, this is the final decision recorded by the teacher once the point haggling is finished.
- *Proposal Outline.* This is where the student will tell you everything about the product he or she intends to complete. These questions should be completed in such a way that you can really picture what the student is planning to complete. This also shows you that the student knows what he or she plans to complete.
  - *What specific topic or idea will you learn about?* Students need to be specific here. It is not acceptable to write "science" or "reading." This is where students look at the objectives of the lesson and choose which objective their product demonstrates.
  - *What criteria should be used to grade it?* Although there are rubrics for all of the products that the students might create, it is important for the students to explain what criteria are most important to evaluate the product. The student may indicate that the rubric being used for all of the predetermined products is fine; however, he or she may also want to add other criteria here.
  - *What will your product look like?* It is important that this response be as detailed as possible. If a student cannot express what it will look like, then he or she has probably not given the free-choice plan enough thought.
  - *What materials will you need from the teacher to create this product?* This is an important consideration. Sometimes students do not have the means to purchase items for their project. This can be negotiated as well, but if you ask what students may need, they will often develop even grander ideas for their free choice.

Chapter 2

How to Use Menus in the Inclusive Classroom

There are different ways to use instructional menus in the inclusive classroom. In order to decide how to implement each menu, the following questions should be considered: How much prior knowledge of the topic being taught do the students have before the unit or lesson begins, how confident are your students in making choices and working independently, and how much intellectually appropriate information is readily available for students to obtain on their own? After considering these questions, there are a variety of ways to use menus in the classroom.

Building Background Knowledge

> "I have students with so many different experiences—sometimes I spend a lot more time than I allotted to review and get everyone up to speed before we get started."
>
> *—Seventh-grade social studies teacher*

DOI: 10.4324/9781003234227-2

There are many ways to use menus in the classroom. One way that is often overlooked is using menus to review or build background knowledge before a unit begins. This is frequently used when students have had exposure to upcoming content in the past, perhaps during the previous year's instruction or through similar life experiences. In reality, most middle school students have had exposure to the basic information needed in their classes; however, students may not remember the details of the content well enough to proceed with the upcoming unit immediately. A shorter menu covering the background or previous year's objectives can be provided in the weeks prior to the new unit so that students have the opportunity to recall and engage with the information in a meaningful way. They will then be ready to take their knowledge to a deeper level during the unit. For example, 2 weeks before beginning a novel from a certain genre, the teacher may select a short menu on the characteristics of that genre, knowing that the students have covered the content in the past and should be able to successfully work independently on the menu by engaging their prior knowledge. Students work on products from the menu as anchor activities and homework throughout the 2 weeks preceding the beginning of the novel, with all products being submitted prior to the novel's initiation. This way, the students have been in the appropriate "genre frame of mind" independently for 2 weeks and are ready to begin their specific novel.

Enrichment and Supplemental Activities

> "I wanted to start allowing some choice in my novel projects, so I chose a menu that matched each genre. It really worked well—the students worked on their projects every day when they had time."
>
> *—Sixth-grade language arts teacher*

Using the menus for enrichment and supplementary activities is the most common way of using menus. In this case, the students usually do not have a lot of background knowledge, and information about the topic may not be readily available to all students. The teacher will introduce the menu and the activities at the beginning of a unit. The teacher then will progress through the content at the normal rate using his or her curricular materials, periodically allowing class and homework time throughout the unit for students to work on their menu choices to supplement a deeper understanding of the lessons being taught. This method is very effective, as it incorporates an immediate use for the content the teacher is covering. For example, at the beginning of a unit on expository writing, the teacher may introduce the menu with the explanation that students may not yet have all of the knowledge needed to complete their choices. During the unit, however, more content will be provided, and the students will be prepared to work on new choices. If students want to work ahead, they can certainly find the information on their own, but that is not required. Although some students often see this as a challenge and will begin to investigate concepts mentioned in the menu before the teacher has discussed them, other students begin to develop questions about the concepts and are ready to ask them when the teacher covers the material. This helps build an immense pool of background knowledge and possible content questions before the topic is even discussed in the classroom. As teachers, we constantly fight the battle of trying to get students to read ahead or come to class already prepared for discussion. By introducing a menu at the beginning of a unit and allowing students to complete products as instruction progresses, we encourage the students to naturally investigate the information and come to class prepared without having to make preparation a separate requirement.

Mainstream Instructional Activities

> "On your suggestion, I tried using the Game Show menu with my geometry unit because I had 3 days of instruction that the students knew well and could work on independently. They really responded to the independence."
>
> *—Eighth-grade math teacher*

Another option for using menus in the classroom is to replace certain curricular activities the teacher uses to teach the specified content. In this case, the students may have some limited background knowledge about the content and have information readily available for them among their classroom resources. This situation allows the teacher to pick and choose which aspects of the content need to be directly taught to the students in large or small groups and which can be appropriately learned and reinforced through product menus. The unit is then designed using formal instructional large-group lessons, smaller informal group lessons, and specific menu days during which the students use the menu to reinforce their prior knowledge. In order for this option to be effective, the teacher must feel very comfortable with the students' prior knowledge level and their readiness to work independently. Another variation on this method is using the menus to drive station activities. Stations have many different functions in the middle school classroom. They can contain activities that are best completed individually to reinforce the content being taught, or—a more common occurrence in middle school—they can allow students access to products or activities that may include specialized resources. Many classrooms may not have enough supplies or resources to set up eight versions of the same activity; however, by making different "resource-heavy" activities available at stations, students can experience the content while the teacher may only need one set-up of each activity.

Mini-Lessons

> "I have so many different levels in my classroom, using menus with mini-lessons has been a life saver. I can actually work with small groups, and everyone else doesn't run wild!"
>
> —*Eighth-grade math teacher*

Yet another option for menus is to use them with mini-lessons, with the menus driving the accompanying classroom activities. This method is best used when the majority of the students have similar amounts of knowledge about the topic. The teacher can design 15–20-minute mini-lessons in which students quickly review basic concepts that are already familiar to them and are then exposed to the new content in a short and concise way. Then students are turned loose to choose an activity on the menu to show that they understand the concept. The Game Show menu usually works very well with this method of instruction, as the topics across the top usually lend themselves to these mini-lessons. It is important that the students either have some prior knowledge of the content or are effective at working independently, because the lesson cycle is shorter in this use of menus. Using menus in this way does shorten the amount of time teachers have to use the guided practice step of the lesson, so all instruction and examples should be carefully selected. By using the menus in this way, the teacher avoids the one-size-fits-all independent practice portion of the lesson. If there are still a few students struggling, they can be pulled into a small-group situation while the other students work on their choices from the menu. Another important consideration is the independence level of the students. In order for this use of menus to be effective, students will need to be able to work independently for up to 30 minutes after the mini-lesson. Because students are often interested in the product they have chosen, this is not a critical issue, but it is still one worth mentioning as teachers consider how they would like to use various menus in their classrooms.

Introducing and Using Leveled Menus With Students

> "That's not fair . . ."
>
> *—A middle school student somewhere in the world, this very minute*

The menus in this book are tiered versions of the menus found in its companion series, Differentiating Instruction With Menus. Although the topics and objectives are alike, these menus may have different values assigned to the same tasks, slightly different wording for similar tasks, the same product options in a menu of a different format, or even tasks that are only available on certain menus. All of these minor modifications make certain menus more appropriate for different students based on their readiness, interests, and ability levels.

As we all know, middle school students tend to compare answers, work, and ideas, and the same goes for their menu choices. Although students may notice the slight aforementioned differences, it may not be an issue when students are working in ability groups, as students are comfortable with not having the exact same options as their classmates. It may also not be an issue when the menus are presented in a matter-of-fact manner, as everyone is getting a menu that was especially chosen for him or her, so students may notice some differences between their menus. Students should rest assured that target numbers (e.g., a goal of 100 points must be met to receive a 100%) is equal for all of the menus provided, and that the activities most often preferred by students are found on all of the menus. Students should also know that most of the menus have a free-choice proposal option, so if they really want to do one of the activities found on another menu in the classroom, they are welcome to submit a free-choice proposal form in order to complete that activity. By presenting tiered menus with confidence and by making it clear that each menu is selected specifically for each student, you can make students much more willing to accept the system and proceed within the confines that you have set.

That being said, you may still have a few students who say, in that dreaded nasal, accusatory, middle schooler's tone: "That's still not fair!" When I first starting using leveled menus with my eighth graders, I heard a few comments like this. They quickly dissipated with my standard and practiced responses. Of course, the first response (which they do not always appreciate) is that fair is not the same as equal. I know students do not like to hear this response, as it is patently true and therefore difficult to dispute. Secondly, I remind students that everyone has different strengths, and the menus are distributed in order to emphasize students' strengths. Again, they know this; they just do not like to acknowledge it. Lastly, if the students are being especially surly, I sometimes have to play the "parent card," meaning that I am the teacher and therefore have the right to do what I feel is best for each student. This last option is non-negotiable, and although students may not like it, they understand the tone and sentiment, as they have usually experienced it at home.

The bottom line when it comes to tiered menus is that students will respond to the use of different menus within a classroom based on how the teacher presents or reacts to the menus. In the past, when I have used different formats, I have addressed the format or obvious differences in a matter-of-fact manner, by saying things such as, "I have spiced things up with this menu and have three different ones that I will pass out. You may receive one that is different than your neighbor's, but whichever one you receive is going to be lots of fun for you!" Other times, when the menus are very similar in their formats and graphics, I simply distribute them and address concerns when they are brought up. For the most part, students are more likely to simply go with what they have been given when the differences in menus are presented confidently, without being open to debate or complaint.

CHAPTER 3

Guidelines for Products

> "I got to do a play! In math!"
>
> —*Seventh-grade student*

This chapter outlines the different types of products included in the featured menus, as well as the guidelines and expectations for each. It is very important that students know exactly what the expectations of a completed product are when they choose to work on it. By discussing these expectations before students begin and having the information readily available ahead of time, you will limit the frustration on everyone's part.

$1 Contract

> "The $1 contract sure cuts out those late-night trips to buy supplies for [my son's] products!"
>
> —*Sixth-grade teacher and parent of a middle schooler*

DOI: 10.4324/9781003234227-3

$1 Contract

I did not spend more than $1.00 on my ______________________________.

____ ________________

Student Signature Date

My child, ______________________, did not spend more than $1.00 on the product he or she created.

____ ________________

Parent Signature Date

Figure 3.1. $1 contract.

Consideration should be given to the cost of creating the products featured on any menu. The resources available to students vary within a classroom, and students should not be graded on the amount of materials they can purchase to make a product look better. These menus are designed to equalize the resources students have available. The materials for most products are available for less than a dollar and can often be found in a teacher's classroom as part of the classroom supplies. If a product requires materials from the student, there is a $1 contract as part of the product criteria. This is a very important piece in the explanation of the product. First of all, by limiting the amount of money a child can spend, teachers create an equal amount of resources for all students. Second, this practice actually encourages a more creative product. When students are limited by the amount of materials they can readily purchase, they often have to use materials from home in new and unique ways. Figure 3.1 is a sample of the contract that has been used many times in my classroom with various products.

The Products

Table 3.1 contains a list of the products used in this book, along with ideas for other products that students may choose to develop as free-choice activities. These products were chosen for their flexibility in meet-

Table 3.1

Products

Visual	Kinesthetic	Auditory
Acrostic	Board Game	Children's Book
Advertisement	Bulletin Board Display	Commercial/Infomercial
Book Cover	Class Game	Game Show
Brochure/Pamphlet	Commercial/Infomercial	Interview
Bulletin Board Display	Concentration Cards	News Report
Cartoon/Comic Strip	Cross-Cut Diagram/Model	Oral Presentation of Created Product
Children's Book	Diorama	Play/Skit
Class Lesson—Written Only	Experiment	PowerPoint—Speaker
Collage	Flipbook	Puppet
Collection	Folded Quiz Book	Song/Rap
Cross-Cut Diagram/Model	Mobile	Speech
Crossword Puzzle	Model	Student-Taught Lesson
Data Table	Mural	Video
Drawing	Museum Exhibit	You Be the Person Presentation
Essay	Play/Skit	
Folded Quiz Book	Product Cube	
Graph	Puppet	
Graphic Novel	Quiz Board	
Greeting Card	Sculpture	
Instruction Card	Student-Taught Lesson	
Journal/Diary	Three-Dimensional Timeline	
Letter	Trophy	
Map	Video	
Mind Map		
Newspaper Article		
Paragraph		
Pie Graph		
Poster		
PowerPoint—Stand Alone		
Questionnaire		
Quiz		
Recipe Card		
Scrapbook		
Story		
Summary		
Survey		
Three Facts and a Fib		
Trading Cards		
Venn Diagram		
Video		
WebQuest		
Windowpane		
Worksheet		

ing different learning styles, as well as for being products many teachers are already using in their classrooms. They have been arranged by learning style—visual, kinesthetic, or auditory—and each menu has been designed to include products from all of these learning styles. Of course, some of the products may represent more than one style of learning, depending on how they are presented or implemented. Some of these products are featured in the menus more often than others, but students may choose the less common products as free-choice options.

Product Frustrations

One of the biggest frustrations that accompany the use of these various products on menus is the barrage of questions about the products themselves. Students can become so wrapped up in the products and the criteria for creating them that they do not focus on the content being presented. This is especially true when menus are introduced to the class. Students can spend an exorbitant amount of time asking the teacher about the products mentioned on the menu. When this happens, what should have been a 10–15-minute menu introduction turns into 45–50 minutes of discussion about product expectations. In order to facilitate the introduction of the menu products, teachers may consider showing students examples of the product(s) from the previous year. Although this can be helpful, it can also lead to additional frustration on the part of both the teacher and the students. Some students may not feel that they can produce a product as nice, as big, as special, or as (you fill in the blank) as the example, or when shown an example, students might interpret that as meaning that the teacher would like something exactly like the one he or she showed to students. To avoid this situation, I would propose that when using examples, the example students are shown be a "blank" one that demonstrates how to create only the shell of the product. If an example of a windowpane is needed, for instance, students might be shown a blank piece of paper that is divided into six panes. The students can then take the skeleton of the product and make it their own as they create their own version of the windowpane using their information.

Product Guidelines

Most frustrations associated with products can be addressed proactively through the use of standardized, predetermined product guidelines, to be shared with students prior to the creation of any products.

These product guidelines are designed in a specific yet generic way, such that any time throughout the school year that the students select a product, that product's guidelines will apply. A beneficial side effect of using set guidelines for a product is the security it creates. Students are often reticent to try something new, as doing so requires taking a risk. Traditionally, when students select a product, they ask questions about creating it, hope they remember and understood all of the details, and turn it in. It can be quite a surprise when they receive the product back and realize that it was not complete or was not what was expected. As you can imagine, students may not want to take the risk on something new the next time; they often prefer to do what they know and be successful. Through the use of product guidelines, students can begin to feel secure in their choices before they start working on new products. If they are not feeling secure, they tend to stay within their comfort zone.

The product guidelines for menu products included in this book, as well as some potential free-choice options, are presented in an easy-to-read card format (see Figure 3.2). (The guidelines for some products, such as summaries, are omitted because teachers often have their own criteria for these products.) Once the products and/or menus have been selected, there are many options available to share this information.

There really is no one right way to share the product guideline information with your students. It all depends on their abilities and needs. Some teachers choose to duplicate and distribute all of the product guidelines pages to students at the beginning of the year so that each child has his or her own copy while working on products. As another option, a few classroom sets can be created by gluing each product guideline card onto a separate index card, hole punching the corner of each card, and placing all of the cards on a metal ring. These ring sets can be placed in a central location or at stations where students can borrow and return them as they work on their products. This allows for the addition of products as they are introduced. Some teachers prefer to introduce product guidelines as students experience products on their menus. In this case, product guidelines from the menu currently assigned can be enlarged, laminated, and posted on a bulletin board for easy access during classroom work. Some teachers may choose to reproduce each menu's specific product guidelines on the back of the menu. No matter which method teachers choose to share the information with the students, they will save themselves a lot of time and frustration by having the product guidelines available for student reference (e.g., "Look at your product guidelines—I think that will answer your question").

Acrostic	Advertisement	Board Game
• Must be at least 8.5" by 11" • Neatly written or typed • Target word written down the left side of the paper • Each descriptive phrase chosen must begin with one of the letters from the target word • Each descriptive phrase chosen must be related to the target word	• Must be at least 8.5" by 11" • A slogan should be included • Color picture of item or service should be included • Include price, if appropriate • Can be created on the computer	• At least four thematic game pieces • At least 20 colored/thematic squares • At least 15 question/activity cards • Include a thematic title on the board • Include a complete set of rules for playing the game • At least the size of an open file folder
Book Cover	**Brochure/Pamphlet**	**Bulletin Board Display**
• Front cover—title, author, image • Front inside flap—paragraph summary of the book • Back inside flap—brief biography of author with at least three details • Back cover—your comments about the book • Spine—title and author	• Must be at least 8.5" by 11" • Must be in three-fold format; front fold has the title and picture • Must have both pictures and written text • Information should be in paragraph form with at least five facts included • Can be created on computer	• Must fit within assigned space on bulletin board or wall • Must include at least five details • Must have a title • Must have at least five different elements (e.g., posters, papers, questions) • Must have at least one interactive element that engages the reader
Cartoon/Comic Strip	**Children's Book**	**Class Game**
• Must be at least 8.5" by 11" • Must have at least six cells • Must have meaningful dialogue • Must include color	• Must have a cover with book's title and student's name as author • Must have at least 10 pages • Each page should have an illustration to accompany the story • Neatly written or typed • Can be created on the computer	• Game should allow all class members to participate • Must have only a few, easy-to-understand rules • Can be a new variation on a current game • Must have multiple questions • Must provide answer key before game is played • Must be approved by teacher before being played

Figure 3.2. Product guidelines.

<table>
<tr>
<td>Class Lesson—Written Only
(Note: For a class lesson that is presented, use the student-taught lesson rubric.)
• Is original—do not just print or copy an activity as is
• States the objectives that will be taught
• Includes at least one warm-up question
• Presents the information in a clear way
• Includes all of the important information
• Has a way for students to practice the content
• Includes a quiz or method of assessment</td>
<td>Collage
• Must be at least 8.5" by 11"
• Pictures must be cut neatly from magazines or newspapers (no clip art from the computer or the Internet)
• Label items as required in task</td>
<td>Collection
• Contains number of items stated in task
• All items must fit in the space designated by the teacher
• All items must be brought to class in a box or bag
• No living things!</td>
</tr>
<tr>
<td>Commercial/Infomercial
• Must be 1–2 minutes in length
• Script must be turned in before the commercial is presented
• Can be presented live to an audience or recorded
• Should have props or some form of costume(s)
• Can include more than one person</td>
<td>Concentration Cards
• At least 20 index cards (10 matching sets) must be made
• Both pictures and words can be used
• Information should be placed on just one side of each card
• Include an answer key that shows the matches
• All cards must be submitted in a carrying bag</td>
<td>Cross-Cut Diagram/Model
• Must include a scale to show the relationship between the diagram/model and the actual item
• Must include details for each layer
• If creating a diagram, must also meet the guidelines for a poster
• If creating a model, must also meet the guidelines for a model</td>
</tr>
<tr>
<td>Crossword Puzzle
• At least 20 significant words or phrases should be included
• Develop appropriate clues
• Include puzzle and answer key
• Can be created on the computer</td>
<td>Data Table
• Table and data have proper units, titles, and descriptions
• All data should be recorded neatly and be easy to read
• If created by hand, all lines should be straight and neat</td>
<td>Diorama
• Must be at least 4" by 5" by 8"
• Must be self-standing
• All interior space must be covered with relevant pictures and information
• Name written on the back
• Informational/title card attached to diorama
• $1 contract signed</td>
</tr>
</table>

Figure 3.2. Continued.

Drawing	Essay	Experiment
• Must be at least 8.5" by 11" • Must show what is requested in the task statement • Must include color • Must be neatly drawn by hand • Must have title • Name written on the back	• Neatly written or typed • Must cover the specific topic in detail • Must be at least three paragraphs • Must include resources or bibliography if appropriate	• Includes a hypothesis or purpose • States specific materials for experiment • Includes detailed procedures and data • Includes a written conclusion in paragraph form • Information neatly written or typed as a report
Flipbook	**Folded Quiz Book**	**Game Show**
• Must be at least 8.5" by 11" folded in half • All information or opinions are supported by facts • Created with the correct number of flaps cut into the top • Color is optional • Name written on the back	• Must be at least 8.5" by 11" folded in half • Must have at least 10 questions • Created with the correct number of flaps cut into the top • Questions written or typed neatly on upper flaps • Answers written or typed neatly inside each flap • Color is optional • Name written on the back	• Needs an emcee or host • Must have at least two contestants • Must have at least one regular round and a bonus round • Questions will be content specific • Props can be used, but are not mandatory
Graph	**Graphic Novel**	**Greeting Card**
• Must have a title • Axes must be labeled with units • All data must be clearly represented • Can be created on the computer • If created by hand, must use graph paper	• Should use color • Must tell a story • Should be at least 10 pages in length • Can be created on the computer	• Front—colored pictures, words optional • Front inside—personal note related to topic • Back inside—greeting or saying; must meet product criteria • Back outside—logo, publisher, and price for card

Figure 3.2. Continued.

Instruction Card

- Must be no larger than 5" by 8"
- Created on heavy paper or index card
- Neatly written or typed
- Uses color drawings
- Provides instructions stated in the task

Interview

- Must have at least eight questions about the topic being studied
- Person chosen for interview must be an "expert" and qualified to provide answers
- Questions and answers must be neatly written or typed

Journal/Diary

- Neatly written or typed
- Should include the appropriate number of entries
- Should include a date if appropriate
- Should be written in first person

Letter

- Neatly written or typed
- Uses proper letter format
- At least three paragraphs in length
- Must follow type of letter stated in the menu (e.g., friendly, persuasive, informational)

Map

- Must be at least 8.5" by 11"
- Accurate information is included
- Includes at least 10 relevant locations
- Includes compass rose, legend, scale, and key

Mind Map

- Must be at least 8.5" by 11"
- Uses unlined paper
- Must have one central idea
- Follows the "no more than four" rule—no more than four words coming from any one word
- Should be neatly written or developed using a computer

Mobile

- Includes at least 10 pieces of related information
- Includes color and pictures
- At least three layers of hanging information
- Hangs in a balanced way

Model

- Must be at least 8" by 8" by 12"
- Parts of model must be labeled
- Should be in scale if possible
- Must include a title card
- Name should be permanently written on the model

Mural

- Must be at least 22" x 54"
- Must contain at least five pieces of important information
- Must have colored pictures
- Words are optional, but a title should be included
- Name should be permanently written on the back

Figure 3.2. Continued.

Museum Exhibit	News Report	Newspaper Article
• Should have title for exhibit • Must include at least five "artifacts" • Each artifact must be labeled with a neatly written card • Exhibit must fit within the size assigned • $1 contract required • No expensive or irreplaceable objects in the display	• Must address the who, what, where, when, why, and how of the topic • Script of report must be turned in with project (or before if performance will be live) • Must be either performed live or recorded	• Must be informational in nature • Must follow standard newspaper format • Must include picture with caption that supports article • At least three paragraphs in length • Neatly written or typed
Paragraph	**Pie Graph**	**Play/Skit**
• Neatly written or typed • Must have topic sentence, at least three supporting sentences or details, and a concluding sentence • Must use appropriate vocabulary and follow grammar rules	• Must have a title • Must have a label for each area or be color coded with a key • Must include the percentages for each area of the graph • Calculations must be provided if needed to create the pie graph • Should be created neatly by hand or using a computer	• Must be 4–6 minutes in length • Script must be turned in before play is presented • May be presented to an audience or recorded for future showing • Should have props or some form of costume(s) • Can include more than one person
Poster	**PowerPoint—Speaker**	**PowerPoint—Stand Alone**
• Should be the size of a standard poster board • Includes at least five pieces of important information • Must have title • Must contain both words and pictures • Name written on the back • Bibliography included as needed	• At least 10 informational slides and one title slide with student's name • No more than two words per page • Slides must have color and no more than one graphic per page • Animations are optional but should not distract from information being presented • Presentation should be timed and flow with the speech being given	• At least 10 informational slides and one title slide with student's name • No more than 10 words per page • Slides must have color and no more than one graphic per page • Animations are optional but should not distract from information being presented

Figure 3.2. Continued.

Product Cube	Puppet	Questionnaire
• All six sides of the cube must be filled with information • Neatly written or typed • Name must be printed neatly on the bottom of one of the sides • Should be submitted flat for grading	• Puppet should be handmade and must have a moveable mouth • A list of supplies used to make the puppet must be turned in with the puppet • $1 contract signed • If used in a puppet show, must also meet the criteria for a play	• Neatly written or typed • Include at least 10 questions with possible answers, and at least one answer that requires a written response • Questions must be helpful to gathering information on the topic being studied
Quiz	**Quiz Board**	**Recipe Card**
• Must be at least a half sheet of paper long • Neatly written or typed • Must cover the specific topic in detail • Must include at least five questions including a short answer question • Must have at least one graphic • An answer key must be turned in with the quiz	• Must have at least five questions • Must have at least five answers • Should use a system with lights • Should be no larger than a poster board • Holiday lights can be used • $1 contract signed	• Must be written neatly or typed on a piece of paper or an index card • Must have a list of ingredients with measurement for each • Must have numbered steps that explain how to make the recipe
Scrapbook	**Sculpture**	**Song/Rap**
• Cover of scrapbook must have a meaningful title and student's name • Must have at least five themed pages • Each page will have at least one meaningful picture • All photos must have captions	• Must be no larger than 24" tall • Must use recycled materials • Must be created from the number of items given in the task • If appropriate, $1 contract must be submitted with sculpture • Creator's name should be permanently written on the base or bottom	• Words must make sense • Can be presented to an audience or taped • Written words must be turned in before performance or with taped song • Should be at least 2 minutes in length

Figure 3.2. Continued.

Speech	Story	Survey
• Must be at least 2 minutes in length • Should not be read from written paper • Note cards can be used • Written speech must be turned in before speech is presented • Voice must be clear, loud, and easy to understand	• Must have all of the elements of a well-written story (setting, characters, conflict, rising action, and resolution) • Must be appropriate length to allow for story elements • Neatly written or typed	• Must have at least five questions related to the topic • Must include at least one adult respondent who is not your teacher • The respondent must sign the survey • Information gathered and conclusions drawn from the survey should be written or presented graphically
Three-Dimensional Timeline	**Three Facts and a Fib**	**Trading Cards**
• Must be no bigger than standard-size poster board • Must be divided into equal time units • Must contain at least 10 important dates and have at least 2 sentences explaining why each date is important • Must have a meaningful object securely attached beside each date to represent that date • Must be able to explain how each object represents each date	• Can be written, typed, or created using PowerPoint • Must include exactly four statements: three true statements and one false statement • False statement should not obvious • Brief paragraph should be included that explains why the fib is false	• Include at least 10 cards • Each card must be at least 3" by 5" • Each should have a colored picture • Includes at least three facts on the subject of the card • Cards must have information on both sides • All cards must be submitted in a carrying bag
Trophy	**Venn Diagram**	**Video**
• Must be at least 6" tall • Must have a base with the name of the person getting the trophy and the name of the award written neatly or typed on it • Top of trophy must be appropriate and represent the award • Name should be written on the bottom of the award • Must be an originally designed trophy (avoid reusing a trophy from home)	• Must be at least 8.5" by 11" • Shapes should be thematic and neatly drawn • Must have a title for entire diagram and a title for each section • Must have at least six items in each section of the diagram • Name written on the back	• Use VHS, DVD, or Flash format • Turn in a written plan with project • Students will need to arrange their own way to record the video or allow teacher at least 3 days notice to set up recording • Covers important information about the project • Name written on the video label

Figure 3.2. Continued.

WebQuest	Windowpane	Worksheet
• Must quest through at least three high-quality websites • Websites should be linked in the document • Can be submitted in a Word or PowerPoint document • Includes at least three questions for each website • Must address the topic	• Must be at least 8.5" by 11" unlined paper • Must include at least six squares • Each square must include both a picture and words that should be neatly written or typed • All pictures should be both creative and meaningful • Name should be written on the bottom right-hand corner of the front of the windowpane	• Must be 8.5" by 11" • Neatly written or typed • Must cover the specific topic or question in detail • Must have at least one graphic • An answer key will be turned in with the worksheet
You Be the Person Presentation • Take on the role of the person • Cover at least five important facts about the life of the person • Must be 3–5 minutes in length • Script must be turned in before information is presented • Should be presented to an audience with the ability to answer questions while in character • Must have props or some form of costume		

Figure 3.2. Continued.

One of the most commonly used products in a language arts classroom is the story map. The story map is a quick and effective way for a student to dissect a story and show that he or she can identify and analyze the important parts of the story. Story maps are an option for some of the menus provided in this book. Two examples, a more basic version (▲) (see Figure 3.3) and an on-level version (●) (see Figure 3.4), are provided. However, teachers who have a favorite format that students are accustomed to should feel free to use their own.

Story Map

▲

Title and Author	Setting

Main Characters

Write at least three traits for each main character.

Supporting Characters

Write one sentence about why each supporting character is important to the story.

Problem

Major Events in the Story

Solution

Figure 3.3. Story map.

Story Map

Title and Author	Setting

Main Characters

For each main character, write at least three traits and a quote from the story to support your chosen traits.

Supporting Characters

Write one sentence about why each supporting character is important to the story.

Problem

Figure 3.4. Story map.

Story Map

Major Events in the Story

Resolution

Figure 3.4. Continued.

Chapter 4

Rubrics

> "[Using menus,] I frequently end up with more papers and products to grade than with a unit taught in the traditional way. Luckily, rubrics speed up the process."
>
> *—Eighth-grade teacher*

The most common reason teachers feel uncomfortable with menus is the need for equal grading. Teachers often feel that it is easier to grade the same type of product made by all of the students than to grade a large number of different products, none of which looks like any other. The great equalizer for hundreds of different products is a generic rubric that can cover all of the important qualities of an excellent product.

DOI: 10.4324/9781003234227-4

All-Purpose Rubric

Figure 4.1 is an example of a rubric that has been classroom tested with the menus included in this book. This rubric can be used with any point value activity presented in a menu, as there are five criteria and the columns represent full points, half points, and no points.

There are different ways that this rubric can be shared with students. Some teachers prefer to provide it when a menu is presented to students. The rubric can be reproduced on the back of the menu along with its guidelines. The rubric can also be given to students to keep in their folders with their product guideline cards so they always know the expectations as they complete projects throughout the school year. Some teachers prefer to keep a master copy for themselves and post an enlarged copy of the rubric on a bulletin board, or provide one copy for parents during open house so that they understand how their children's menu products will be graded.

No matter how the rubric is shared with students, the first time they see this rubric, it should be explained to them in detail, especially the last column, titled "Self." It is very important that students self-evaluate their projects. This column can provide a unique perspective on the project as it is being graded. Note: This rubric was designed to be specific enough that students will understand the criteria the teacher is seeking, but general enough that they can still be as creative as they like while making their products.

Student-Taught Lesson and Oral Presentation Rubrics

Although the all-purpose product rubric can be used for all activities, there are two situations that warrant a special rubric: student-taught lessons and oral presentations. These situations have many fine details that must be considered separately.

Student-taught lessons can cause stress for both students and teachers. Teachers would often like to allow students to teach their fellow classmates, but they are not comfortable with the grading aspect of the assignment. Rarely do students understand all of the components that go into designing an effective lesson. This student-taught lesson rubric (see Figure 4.2) helps focus the student on the important aspects of a well-designed lesson and allows teachers to make the evaluation more subjective.

All-Purpose Rubric

Name: ____________________

Criteria	Excellent (Full Credit)	Good (Half Credit)	Poor (No Credit)	Self
Content Is the content of the product well chosen?	Content chosen represents the best choice for the product. Information or graphics are well chosen and related to content.	Information or graphics are related to content, but are not the best choice for the product.	Information or graphics presented do not appear to be related to the topic or task.	
Completeness Is everything included in the product?	All information needed is included. Product meets the product criteria and the criteria of the task as stated.	Some important information is missing. Product meets the product criteria and the criteria of the task as stated.	Most important information is missing. The product does not meet the task or does not meet the product criteria.	
Creativity Is the product original?	Presentation of information is from a new perspective. Graphics are original. Product includes elements of fun and interest.	Presentation of information is from a new perspective. Graphics are not original. Product has elements of fun and interest.	There is no evidence of new thoughts or perspectives in the product.	
Correctness Is all of the information included correct?	All information presented in the product is correct and accurate.		Any portion of the information presented in the product is incorrect.	
Communication Is the information in the product well communicated?	All information is neat and easy to read. Product is in appropriate format and shows significant effort. Oral presentations are easy to understand and presented with fluency.	Most of the product is neat and easy to read. Product is in appropriate format and shows significant effort. Oral presentations are easy to understand, with some fluency.	The product is not neat and easy to read or the product is not in the appropriate format. It does not show significant effort. Oral presentation was not fluent or easy to understand.	
			Total Grade:	

Figure 4.1. All-purpose product rubric.

Student-Taught Lesson Rubric

Name: ______________________

Parts of Lesson	Excellent	Good	Fair	Poor	Self
Prepared and Ready All materials and lesson ready at start of class period, from warm-up to conclusion of lesson.	**10** Everything is ready to present.	**6** Lesson is present, but small amount of scrambling.	**3** Lesson is present, but major scrambling.	**0** No lesson ready or missing major components.	
Understanding Presenter understands the material well. Students understand information presented.	**20** All information is correct and in correct format.	**12** Presenter understands; 25% of students do not.	**4** Presenter understands; 50% of students do not.	**0** Presenter is confused.	
Complete Includes all significant information from section or topic.	**15** Includes all important information.	**10** Includes most important information.	**2** Includes less than 50% of the important information.	**0** Information is not related.	
Practice Includes some way for students to practice or access the information.	**20** Practice present; well chosen.	**10** Practice present; can be applied effectively.	**5** Practice present; not related or best choice.	**0** No practice or students are confused.	
Interest/Fun Most of the class is involved, interested, and participating.	**15** Everyone interested and participating.	**10** 75% actively participating.	**5** Less than 50% actively participating.	**0** Everyone off task.	
Creativity Information presented in an imaginative way.	**20** Wow, creative! I never would have thought of that!	**12** Good ideas!	**5** Some good pieces but general instruction.	**0** No creativity; all lecture, notes, or worksheet.	
				Total Grade:	

Your Topic/Objective:

Comments:

Don't Forget:
All copy requests and material requests must be made at least 24 hours in advance.

Figure 4.2. Student-taught lesson rubric.

Within the language arts curriculum, considerable emphasis is placed on presenting information in a spoken manner. The oral presentation rubrics assist with this goal. Two rubrics are included: one for the evaluation of the speaker by the teacher (see Figure 4.3), and one for feedback from the students (see Figure 4.4). This student feedback rubric is included in order to encourage active participation on the part of student observers. This student feedback should always be given in a positive manner. When my students give oral presentations, they actually seem to value their peers' feedback even more than mine!

When using the oral presentation rubrics, please note that the rubric adds to 100 points. With the exception of the 100-point home run option offered on a baseball menu, no single menu products are worth 100 points. In my classroom, I simply explained to my students that the 100-point total was the percentage of total points possible for the activity. If a speech was worth 30 points, then a score of 100 on the oral presentation rubric would earn them 100% of the 30 points, whereas an 80 on the rubric would result in 24 points out of 30. Usually, simply by using the rubric, the students give presentations of a higher quality, as they are made more aware of the elements of a successful presentation.

Student Presentation Rubric

Criteria	Excellent	Good	Fair	Poor	Self
Content Complete Did the presentation include everything it should?	**30** Presentation included all important information about topic being presented.	**20** Presentation covered most of the important information, but one key idea was missing.	**10** Presentation covered some of the important information, but more than one key idea was missing.	**0** Presentation covered information, but the information was trivial or fluff.	
Content Correct Was the information presented accurate?	**30** All information presented was accurate.	**20** All information presented was correct, with a few unintentional errors that were quickly corrected.		**0** Any information presented was not correct.	
Prop Did the speaker have at least one prop that was directly related to the presentation?	**20** Presenter had a prop and it complemented the presentation.	**12** Presenter had a prop, but it was not the best choice.	**4** Presenter had a prop, but there was no clear reason for it.	**0** Presenter had no prop.	
Content Consistent Did the speaker stay on topic?	**10** Presenter stayed on topic 100% of the time.	**7** Presenter stayed on topic 90%–99% of the time.	**4** Presenter stayed on topic 80%–89% of the time.	**0** It was hard to tell what the topic was.	
Flow Was the speaker familiar and comfortable with the material so that it flowed well?	**10** Presentation flowed well. Speaker did not stumble over words.	**7** Presenter had some flow problems, but they did not distract from information.	**4** Some flow problems interrupted the presentation, and presenter seemed flustered.	**0** Constant flow problems occurred, and information was not presented so that it could be understood.	
				Total Grade:	

Figure 4.3. Oral presentation rubric.

Topic: ______________________ **Student's Name:** ______________________

On a scale of 1–10, rate the following areas:

Content (How in depth was the information? How well did the speaker know the information? Was the information correct? Could the speaker answer questions?)		Give one short reason why you gave this number.
Flow (Did the presentation flow smoothly? Did the speaker appear confident and ready to speak?)		Give one short reason why you gave this number.
Prop (Did the speaker explain his or her prop? Did this choice seem logical? Was it the best choice?)		Give one short reason why you gave this number.

Comments: Below, write two things that you think the presenter did well:

1.

2.

Topic: ______________________ **Student's Name:** ______________________

On a scale of 1–10, rate the following areas:

Content (How in depth was the information? How well did the speaker know the information? Was the information correct? Could the speaker answer questions?)		Give one short reason why you gave this number.
Flow (Did the presentation flow smoothly? Did the speaker appear confident and ready to speak?)		Give one short reason why you gave this number.
Prop (Did the speaker explain his or her prop? Did this choice seem logical? Was it the best choice?)		Give one short reason why you gave this number.

Comments: Below, write two things that you think the presenter did well:

1.

2.

Figure 4.4. Student feedback rubric.

The Menus

How to Use the Menu Pages

Each menu in this section has:

- an introduction page for the teacher;
- a lower level content menu, indicated by a triangle (▲) in the upper right-hand corner;
- an on-level content menu, indicated by a circle (●) in the upper right-hand corner;
- any specific guidelines for the menu; and
- activities mentioned in the menu.

Introduction Pages

The introduction pages are meant to provide an overview of each menu. They are divided into five areas:

1. *Objectives Covered Through These Menus and These Activities.* This area will list all of the objectives that the menus can address. Menus are arranged in such a way that if students complete the guidelines set forth in the instructions for the menus, all of these objectives will be covered. In this book, the objectives are broken

DOI: 10.4324/9781003234227-5

down into the reading objectives and writing objectives covered by each menu.

2. *Materials Needed by Students for Completion.* For each menu, it is expected that the teacher will provide, or students will have access to, the following materials:
   - lined paper;
   - glue;
   - crayons, colored pencils, or markers; and
   - blank 8.5" x 11" white paper.

   The introduction page also includes a list of additional materials that may be needed by students as they complete either menu. Any materials listed that are used in only one of the two menus are designated with the menu's corresponding code (either triangle or circle). Students do have the choice about the menu items they can complete, so it is possible that the teacher will not need all of these materials for every student.
3. *Special Notes on the Use of These Menus.* This section will give any special tips on managing student products as well as any specific modification suggestions. This section will also share any tips to consider for a specific activity.
4. *Time Frame.* Most menus are best used in at least a 1-week time frame. Some are better suited to more than 2 weeks. This section will give an overview about the best time frame for completing the entire menu, as well as options for shorter time periods. If teachers do not have time to devote to an entire menu, they can certainly choose the 1–2-day option for any menu topic students are currently studying.
5. *Suggested Forms.* This is a list of the rubrics, templates, and reproducibles that should be available for students as the menus are introduced. If a menu has a free-choice option, the appropriate proposal form also will be listed here.

Chapter 5

Genres

Note: Instead of including specific novels in this book, I have decided to feature the popular genres discussed in many middle schools. This will allow flexibility for teachers who select their own novels or use multiple concurrent literature groups with different novels of the same genre. By using the menu that matches the genre of the literature, students can analyze their specific novels as well as their corresponding genres.

DOI: 10.4324/9781003234227-6

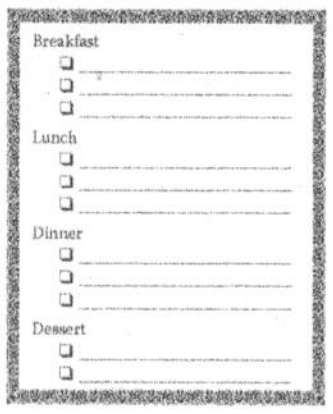

Author Study

Meal Menu ▲ and Tic-Tac-Toe Menu ●

Reading Objectives Covered Through These Menus and These Activities

- Students will compare one literary work with another.
- Students will make and explain inferences based on the written work.
- Students will analyze characters, their relationships, and their importance in the story.
- Students will distinguish between an author's opinion and fact.

Writing Objectives Covered Through These Menus and These Activities

- Students will write to express their feelings, develop ideas, reflect, or problem solve.
- Students will write to inform, explain, describe, or narrate.
- Students will exhibit voice in their writing.
- Students will use vivid language.

Materials Needed by Students for Completion

- Poster board or large white paper
- Materials for bulletin board displays
- Microsoft PowerPoint or other slideshow software
- Scrapbooking materials ▲
- Materials for three-dimensional timelines

Special Notes on the Use of These Menus

This topic has two different menu formats: Meal menu and Tic-Tac-Toe menu. The Meal menu is specifically selected for its meal-oriented, Bloom's-based options, as it is easily broken into manageable bits. The menu can be cut into strips, each strip featuring its own meal, to be given to students. This way, once students have chosen and submitted the breakfast product for grading, they can move on to the lunch strip, and lastly, they can complete the dinner and dessert strips. Because this type of menu is designed to become more advanced as students move through the meals, teachers may choose to provide their students who have special needs with just the meals and save the dessert for enrichment.

These menus allow students to create a bulletin board display. Some classrooms may only have one bulletin board, so the teacher can divide the board into sections, or additional classroom wall or hall space can be sectioned off for the creation of these displays. Students can plan their displays based on the amount of space they are assigned.

Time Frame

- 2–3 weeks—Students are given the menus as the unit is started. As the teacher presents lessons throughout the week, he or she should refer back to the menu options associated with that content. The teacher will go over all of the options for that content and have students place check marks in the boxes that represent the activities they are most interested in completing. If students are using the Tic-Tac-Toe menu form, activities chosen and completed should make a column or row. If students are using the Meal menu form, students will complete one product from each meal, with dessert being an optional enrichment product. When students complete these patterns, they will have completed one activity from each content area, learning style, or level of Bloom's Revised taxonomy.
- 1 week—At the start of the unit, the teacher chooses the three activities he or she feels are most valuable for students. Stations can be set up in the classroom. These three activities are available for student choice throughout the week as regular instruction takes place.
- 1–2 days—The teacher chooses an activity from the menu to use with the entire class.

Suggested Forms

- All-purpose rubric
- Oral presentation rubric
- Student feedback rubric
- Free-choice proposal form

Name:______________________________________ Date:____________________

Author Study

Directions: Choose one activity each for breakfast, lunch, and dinner. Dessert is an activity you can choose to do after you have finished your other meals. All products must be completed by: ________________.

Breakfast

- ❒ Create a three-dimensional timeline of the important events in your author's life that led to his or her career in writing.
- ❒ Write an acrostic for the last name of your author. Using the letters, share important information about your author's life.
- ❒ Create a scrapbook for your author that shares the important events that impacted his or her writing career.

Lunch

- ❒ Create a bulletin board display about your author and other authors who you feel use the same theme as your author. Your display should focus on how your author and the others are alike.
- ❒ Choose an author who writes with a purpose similar to your author's. Create a greeting card that the other author might send to your author to congratulate him or her on a new novel.
- ❒ Create a Venn diagram to compare and contrast your author to another author in our current unit. Be sure to choose your diagram shapes to represent the authors!

Dinner

- ❒ Write a play in which at least two different characters from two different books by your author meet and have an adventure. If your author has only written one book, use characters from that book who do not know each other.
- ❒ Create a children's book about your author and his or her works. Readers should finish your book wanting to read one of your author's books.
- ❒ Free choice—Submit a free-choice proposal about your author's works to your teacher for approval.

Dessert

- ❒ After reading different works by your author, compose a letter that shares your feelings about his or her specific works. Be specific! Locate the address of your author's publisher and send the letter to your author.
- ❒ Choose another author who you feel writes in a way similar to your author. Create a PowerPoint presentation that shows similarities in the authors' choice of characters, themes, plots, and purpose.

Name:______________________________ Date:______________________

Author Study

Directions: Check the boxes you plan to complete. They should form a tic-tac-toe across or down. All products are due by: ______________________.

☐ *The Author's Life* Create a three-dimensional timeline of the significant events in your author's life that led to his or her career in writing.	☐ *The Author's Works* Write an original play in which at least three different characters from three different books by your author meet and have an adventure. If your author has only written one or two books, use three different characters from those.	☐ *The Author's Peers* Choose an author who writes with a purpose similar to your author's. Create a greeting card that the other author might send to your author congratulating him or her on a new novel.
☐ *The Author's Peers* Create a bulletin board display about your author and other authors who you feel use the same theme. Your display should focus on the similarities between your author and the others you have chosen.	☐ **Free Choice: The Author's Life** (Fill out your proposal form before beginning the free choice!)	☐ *The Author's Works* Create a children's book about your author and his or her works. After readers finish your book, they should want to read at least one of your author's books.
☐ *The Author's Works* After reading different works written by your author, compose a letter that shares your feelings about his or her works. Be specific! Locate the address of your author's publisher and send the letter to your author.	☐ *The Author's Peers* Choose another author who you feel writes in a way similar to your author's. Create a PowerPoint presentation that shows similarities in the authors' choice of characters, themes, plots, and purpose.	☐ *The Author's Life* Consider the events in your author's life that have had the greatest impact on his or her works and writing style. Write a newspaper article about the life and writing career of your author.

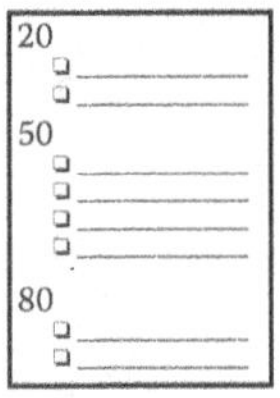

Biographies

20-50-80 Menus

Reading Objectives Covered Through These Menus and These Activities

- Students will make and explain inferences based on a written work.
- Students will make predictions based on what is read.
- Students will show comprehension by retelling or acting out events in a story.
- Students will distinguish between an author's opinion and fact.

Writing Objectives Covered Through These Menus and These Activities

- Students will write to inform, explain, describe, or narrate.
- Students will write to influence or persuade.
- Students will exhibit voice in their writing.

Materials Needed by Students for Completion

- Poster board or large white paper
- Scrapbooking materials ●
- Materials for museum exhibits (e.g., boxes, cards)
- Empty cereal boxes
- Materials for three-dimensional timelines

Time Frame

- 1–2 weeks—Students are given the menus as the unit is started, and the teacher discusses all of the product options on the menus. As the different options are discussed, students will choose products that add to a total of 100 points. As the lessons progress, the teacher and students refer back to the menu options associated with the content being taught.
- 1–2 days—The teacher chooses an activity or product from the menu to use with the entire class.

Suggested Forms

- All-purpose rubric
- Point-based free-choice proposal form

Name:____ Date:_______________________ ▲

Biographies

Directions: Choose at least two activities from the menu below. The activities must total at least 100 points. Place a check mark next to each box to show which activities you will complete. All activities must be completed by: ___________________.

20 Points

- ❒ After reading a biography, choose eight significant events in the life of the person you read about. Using these dates, create a three-dimensional timeline of the person's life.
- ❒ Free choice—Prepare a proposal form and submit your idea for approval.

50 Points

- ❒ Create Three Facts and a Fib about the person in your biography.
- ❒ Create a museum exhibit for the person in your biography. Be sure to include information about the person's life!
- ❒ Design a letter to send to a famous person asking about his or her life and accomplishments. Research the famous person before writing the letter. If the person is still alive, send him or her your letter to see if you receive a response.
- ❒ Create a Venn diagram to compare and contrast the early life of the person in your biography with your own life.

80 Points

- ❒ Write an autobiography about your life and your accomplishments.
- ❒ Famous athletes are not the only people who can be on cereal boxes. Design a cereal box based on your own life. Be creative in its design and include a picture, information about the cereal, and a list of your accomplishments.

Name:____ Date:______________________

Biographies

Directions: Choose at least two activities from the menu below. The activities must total at least 100 points. Place a check mark next to each box to show which activities you will complete. All activities must be completed by: ____________________.

20 Points

- ❒ After reading the biography, choose 10 significant events in the life of the person you read about. Using these dates, create a three-dimensional timeline of the person's life.
- ❒ Create Three Facts and a Fib about the person in your biography.

50 Points

- ❒ Create a museum exhibit for the person in your biography. Include not only information about the person's life, but also his or her impact on society.
- ❒ After researching a famous person of your choice, think about the significant events in his or her life. Create a scrapbook about his or her impact on people's lives.
- ❒ Design a letter to send to a famous person asking about his or her life and accomplishments. Research the famous person before composing the letter so your questions are relevant. If the person is still alive, send him or her your letter to see if you receive a response.
- ❒ Free choice—Prepare a proposal form and submit your idea for approval.

80 Points

- ❒ Write an autobiography about your life and your accomplishments.
- ❒ Famous athletes are not the only people who can be on cereal boxes. Design a cereal box based on your own life. Be creative in its design and include a picture, information about the cereal, and a list of your accomplishments.

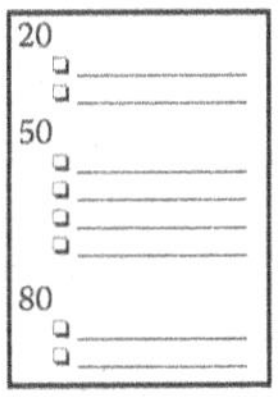

Nonfiction

20-50-80 Menus

Reading Objectives Covered Through These Menus and These Activities

- Students will compare one written work with another.
- Students will use resources and references to build meaning.
- Students will share information gained from reading a nonfiction selection.
- Students will evaluate the information provided in nonfiction sources.

Writing Objectives Covered Through These Menus and These Activities

- Students will write to express their feelings, develop ideas, reflect, or problem solve.
- Students will write to inform, explain, describe, or narrate.
- Students will write to influence or persuade.

Materials Needed by Students for Completion

- Poster board or large white paper
- Graph paper or Internet access (for crossword puzzles) ●
- Materials for museum exhibits (e.g., boxes, cards) ●
- Magazines (for collages)
- Materials for quiz boards (e.g., batteries, holiday lights, aluminum foil, tape) ▲
- Materials for models ▲

Special Notes on the Use of These Menus

The triangle menu offers students the opportunity to create a quiz board. Quiz boards can range from simple to very complex, depending on the knowledge and ability of the student. Quiz boards work best when the teacher creates a "tester" that can be used to check any boards that are submitted. Basic instructions on how to create quiz boards and testers can be found at http://www.cesiscience.org/attachments/article/100/QuizBoardDirections.pdf.

Time Frame

- 1–2 weeks—Students are given the menus as the unit is started, and the teacher discusses all of the product options on the menus. As the

different options are discussed, students will choose products that add to a total of 100 points. As the lessons progress, the teacher and students refer back to the menu options associated with the content being taught.
- 1–2 days—The teacher chooses an activity or product from the menu to use with the entire class.

Suggested Forms
- All-purpose rubric
- Point-based free-choice proposal form

Name:____ Date:______________________ ▲

Nonfiction

Directions: Choose at least two activities from the menu below. The activities must total at least 100 points. Place a check mark next to each box to show which activities you will complete. All activities must be completed by: ______________________.

20 Points

- ❒ Create a collage of pictures related to the topic of your nonfiction selection.
- ❒ Design a quiz board to quiz your classmates about your topic.

50 Points

- ❒ Use facts from your nonfiction selection to create a model. Include a written description of the model.
- ❒ Write a song or rap to help teach others about your topic. It needs to include at least 10 details about your topic.
- ❒ Create a Venn diagram to compare and contrast two things you read about in your nonfiction selection.
- ❒ Write Three Facts and a Fib using the information provided in the nonfiction work you selected.

80 Points

- ❒ Choose two different nonfiction books about your topic. After reading each book, determine which you feel is the better book. Design a book cover for that book. In the editorial comments area, include your reasons for choosing it.
- ❒ Free choice—Prepare a proposal form and submit your idea for approval.

Name:______________________________________ Date:__________________

Nonfiction

Directions: Choose at least two activities from the menu below. The activities must total at least 100 points. Place a check mark next to each box to show which activities you will complete. All activities must be completed by: ____________________.

20 Points

- ❒ Create a collage of pictures and words related to the topic of your nonfiction selection.
- ❒ Write Three Facts and a Fib about your topic.

50 Points

- ❒ Use facts from your nonfiction selection to create a museum exhibit. Include a written description of the objects or photos.
- ❒ Write a song or rap to help teach others about your topic. It needs to include at least 10 details about your topic.
- ❒ Create a brochure that shares important details about your topic, why you chose it, and how it relates to your everyday life.
- ❒ Design a crossword puzzle using information provided in the nonfiction work you selected.

80 Points

- ❒ Choose two different nonfiction books about your topic. After reading each book, determine which you feel is the better book. Design a book cover for that book. In the editorial comments area, include your reasons for choosing it.
- ❒ Free choice—Prepare a proposal form and submit your idea for approval.

Fiction

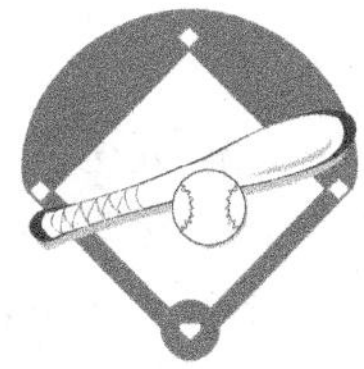

List Menu ▲ and Baseball Menu ●

Reading Objectives Covered Through These Menus and These Activities

- Students will interpret figurative language and multiple-meaning words.
- Students will make and explain inferences based on a written work.
- Students will show comprehension by retelling or acting out events in a story.
- Students will represent textual evidence by using story maps.

Writing Objectives Covered Through These Menus and These Activities

- Students will write to express their feelings, develop ideas, reflect, or problem solve.
- Students will support their responses with textual evidence.
- Students will write to inform, explain, describe, or narrate.
- Students will exhibit voice in their writing.
- Students will use vivid language.

Materials Needed by Students for Completion

- Poster board or large white paper
- Story map template
- Magazines (for collages)
- Materials for dioramas (e.g., shoe boxes, cards)
- Materials for board games (e.g., folders, colored cards)
- Graph paper or Internet access (for crossword puzzles)
- Materials for three-dimensional timelines ●
- Rulers (for comic strips)
- Coat hangers (for mobiles)
- Blank index cards (for mobiles)
- String (for mobiles)
- Microsoft PowerPoint or other slideshow software
- Materials for trophies

Time Frame

- 2–3 weeks—Students are given the menus as the unit is started, and guidelines and point expectations are discussed. Usually, students are expected to complete 100 points. Because these menus cover one topic in depth, the teacher will go over all of the options for the topic being covered and have students place check marks in the boxes next to the activities they are most interested in completing. As instruction continues, activities are completed by students and submitted for grading.

- 1 week—At the beginning of the unit, the teacher chooses one or two higher level activities that can be integrated into whole-group instruction throughout the week.
- 1–2 days—The teacher chooses an activity from an objective to use with the entire class during lesson time.

Suggested Forms

- All-purpose rubric
- Oral presentation rubric
- Student feedback rubric
- Point-based free-choice proposal form

Name:____ Date:________________________ ▲

Fiction: Side 1

Guidelines:

1. You may complete as many of the activities listed as you can within the time period.
2. You may choose any combination of activities.
3. Your goal is 100 points. You may earn up to _____ points extra credit.
4. You may be as creative as you like within the guidelines listed below.
5. You must show your plan to your teacher by ___________________.
6. Activities may be turned in at any time during the working time period. They will be graded and recorded on this sheet as you continue to work, so keep it safe!

If you are using this menu for more than one book, please write the titles and authors of the books you are using below:

____

____

____

Plan to Do	Activity to Complete (Side 1: 10–30 points)	Point Value	Date Completed	Points Earned
	Complete another student's crossword puzzle for a story or novel you have read.	10		
	Create a book cover for your story or novel.	15		
	Create a diorama of your favorite scene in the story or novel.	15		
	Create a folded quiz book about the characters and events in your story or novel.	15		
	Design an acrostic for your favorite character. Use character traits for each letter of his or her name.	15		
	Create a crossword puzzle about the characters, events, and settings of your story or novel.	20		
	Create a quiz that covers the plot, themes, and characters in your story or novel.	20		
	Design a personality collage for two of your favorite characters from the story or novel (they do not have to be main characters). Include at least 10 words for each character.	20		
	Fill in a story map for the story or novel of your choice.	20		
	Using a Venn diagram, compare and contrast two different works written by the author of your story or novel.	20		
	Create a character mobile. Place all of the characters on the mobile and include one trait for each one. Under each trait, select a supporting quote from the story or novel.	30		
	Design a greeting card you could give to a character in your story or novel for something he or she experiences.	30		
	Total number of points you are planning to earn from Side 1.	**Total points earned from Side 1:**		

Name:______________________________ Date:____________________

Fiction: Side 2

Plan to Do	Activity to Complete (Side 2: 35 points and up)	Point Value	Date Completed	Points Earned
	Create a board game to follow the events in your story or novel.	35		
	Create a windowpane with at least 10 panes for the theme of your story or novel. Place quotes from the work in each pane that exemplify how the theme is shown.	35		
	Design an advertisement for your story or novel that encourages your classmates to read it.	35		
	The author of your story or novel is thinking about allowing his or her characters to be used in a new comic strip. Design and draw the comic strip.	35		
	We often wish to know the future. Write a letter to be delivered to a character early on in the story or novel, giving him or her advice for the future.	40		
	Consider the theme, characters, and plot of your story or novel. Write a children's book using the same theme, characters, or plot (choose only one of the three). Do not just retell the story—make it creative!	60		
	The Book Hall of Fame is taking nominations for the best book ever written. Select a story or novel and design a PowerPoint presentation explaining your selection.	60		
	Two of your characters have been nominated for an award. Consider the characters' strengths and actions to decide what award they qualify for. Define the criteria and design a trophy for the award. Using PowerPoint, create an application for both characters that shows the personality traits and achievements that qualify them to win. Be sure to use quotes from the story or novel. Based on the criteria, select the winner and perform his or her acceptance speech.	100		
	Free choice: must be outlined on a proposal form and approved before beginning work.	10–40 points		
	Total number of points you are planning to earn from Side 1.		**Total points earned from Side 1:**	
	Total number of points you are planning to earn from Side 2.		**Total points earned from Side 2:**	
			Grand Total (/100)	

I am planning to complete ____ activities that could earn up to a total of _____ points.

Teacher's initials _______ Student's signature ______________________________

Name:____ Date:______________________

Fiction

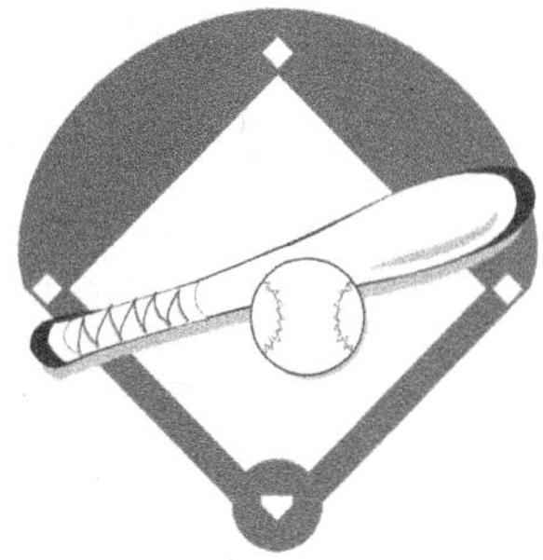

Directions: Look through the following choices and decide how you want to make your game add to 100 points. Singles are worth 10, Doubles are worth 30, Triples are worth 50, and a Home Run is worth 100. Choose any combination you want! Place a check mark next to each choice you are going to complete. Make sure that your points equal 100!

If you are using this menu for more than one book, please write the titles and authors of the books you are using below:

____

____

____

Singles—10 Points Each

- ❐ Fill in a story map for a fictional story or novel of your choice.
- ❐ Create a quiz that covers the plot, themes, and characters in your story or novel.
- ❐ Create a book cover for your story or novel.
- ❐ Design a personality collage for two of your favorite characters from the story or novel (they do not have to be main characters). The collage should contain at least 15 words for each character.
- ❐ Create a diorama of your favorite scene in the story or novel.
- ❐ Write a folded quiz book about the characters and events in your story or novel.
- ❐ Create a three-dimensional timeline that shows the major events in your story or novel.
- ❐ Using a Venn diagram, compare and contrast two different books written by the author of your story or novel.

Doubles—30 Points Each

- ❐ Design an advertisement for your story or novel that encourages your classmates to read it.
- ❐ Create a board game that follows the events in your story or novel and includes questions about decisions the characters made during the novel.
- ❐ The author of your story or novel is contemplating allowing his or her characters to be used in a new comic strip. Design and draw the comic strip.
- ❐ Design a greeting card that you could give to one of your characters for something he or she experienced during the story or novel.
- ❐ We often wish to see into the future and to know what's in store for us. Write a letter to one of your characters, to be delivered early in the story or novel, giving him or her advice that will help the character in the future.

Name:____ Date:_______________________

Doubles—30 Points Each (continued)

- ❒ Create a character mobile. Place all of your characters on the mobile with two traits for each character. Under each trait, select a quote from the story or novel that supports why you chose that trait.
- ❒ Create a windowpane with at least 10 panes for the theme of your story or novel. In each pane, place quotes from different parts of the story or novel that exemplify how the theme is seen throughout the work.

Triples—50 Points Each

- ❒ The Book Hall of Fame is taking nominations for the best book ever written. Design a PowerPoint presentation to submit a book for this honor. Describe your book in detail and explain why it deserves the honor.
- ❒ Consider the theme, characters, and plot of your story or novel. Write a children's book that uses the same theme, characters, or plot (choose only one of the three). Do not just retell the story—make it creative!
- ❒ Two of the characters in your story or novel have been selected as contestants on a local game show. Invent a game show in which they could participate, taking into consideration their abilities and strengths. Perform your game show.

Home Run—100 Points Each

- ❒ Two of your characters have been nominated for a special award. Taking into consideration their strengths and good deeds, determine what type of award this might be. Although both characters may not qualify, define and record the criteria for the award and design a trophy for the award. Using Microsoft PowerPoint or other slideshow software, create an application for both characters that shows their personality traits and achievements that qualify them for the award. Be sure to support each achievement or personality trait with a quote from the story or novel. Based on the criteria, select the winner and perform his or her acceptance speech for your classmates.

I Chose:

________ Singles (10 points each)

________ Doubles (30 points each)

________ Triples (50 points each)

________ Home Run (100 points)

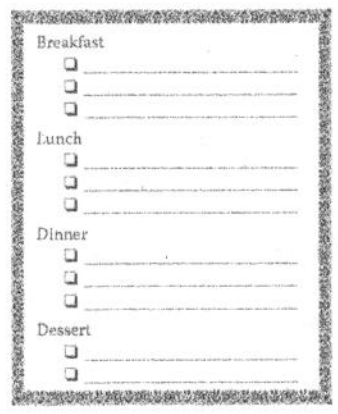

Novel Study

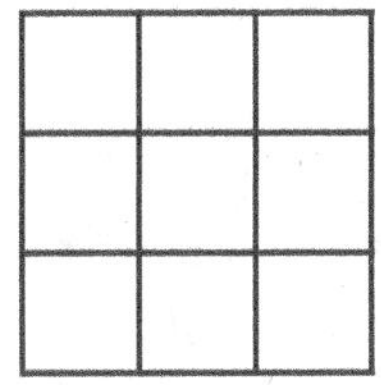

Meal Menu ▲ and Tic-Tac-Toe Menu ●

Reading Objectives Covered Through These Menus and These Activities

- Students will make predictions based on what is read.
- Students will show comprehension by summarizing a story.
- Students will analyze characters, their relationships, and their importance in the story.
- Students will recognize and analyze plot and problem resolution.

Writing Objectives Covered Through These Menus and These Activities

- Students will write to express their feelings, develop ideas, reflect, or problem solve.
- Students will support their responses with textual evidence.
- Students will exhibit voice in their writing.

Materials Needed by Students for Completion

- Poster board or large white paper
- Product cube template
- DVD or VHS recorder (for videos and commercials)
- Materials for bulletin board displays
- Materials for three-dimensional timelines
- Materials for dioramas (e.g., shoe boxes, cards) ▲
- Materials for trophies ▲

Special Notes on the Use of These Menus

This topic has two different menu formats: Meal menu and Tic-Tac-Toe menu. The Meal menu is specifically selected for its meal-oriented, Bloom's-based options, as it is easily broken into manageable bits. The menu can be cut into strips, each strip featuring its own meal, to be given to students. This way, once students have chosen and submitted the breakfast product for grading, they can move on to the lunch strip, and lastly, they can complete the dinner and dessert strips. Because this type of menu is designed to become more advanced as students move through the meals, teachers may choose to provide their students who have special needs with just the meals and save the dessert for enrichment.

These menus give students the opportunity to create a video or commercial. Although students enjoy producing their own videos, there are often difficulties obtaining the equipment and scheduling the use of the video recorder. The menus can be modified by allowing students to act out their videos and commercials (like a play), or if students have the technology, they may wish to produce a webcam or Flash version of their videos and commercials.

Time Frame

- 2–3 weeks—Students are given the menus as the unit is started. As the teacher presents lessons throughout the week, he or she should refer back to the menu options associated with that content. The teacher will go over all of the options for that content and have students place check marks in the boxes that represent the activities they are most interested in completing. If students are using the Tic-Tac-Toe menu form, activities chosen and completed should make a column or row. If students are using the Meal menu form, students will complete one product from each meal, with dessert being an optional enrichment product. When students complete these patterns, they will have completed one activity from each content area, learning style, or level of Bloom's Revised taxonomy.
- 1 week—At the start of the unit, the teacher chooses the three activities he or she feels are most valuable for students. Stations can be set up in the classroom. These three activities are available for student choice throughout the week as regular instruction takes place.
- 1–2 days—The teacher chooses an activity from the menu to use with the entire class.

Suggested Forms

- All-purpose rubric
- Oral presentation rubric
- Student feedback rubric
- Free-choice proposal form

Name:____ Date:______________________ ▲

Novel Study

Directions: Choose one activity each for breakfast, lunch, and dinner. Dessert is an activity you can choose to do after you have finished your other meals. All products must be completed by: ____________________.

Breakfast

❒ Create a three-dimensional timeline for the main character in your novel. Include at least one date before the novel begins.

❒ Create a mind map for the characters in your novel. Include information about each character and the characters' relationships.

❒ Create a greeting card that one character might give another character in your novel. Be sure to include a personal note based on the novel.

Lunch

❒ Complete this statement with just one word: Everyone thinks the main character of my novel is __________________. Create a cube using the six best quotes from your novel that prove your statement is true.

❒ Choose two quotes from your novel that describe the setting. Use these quotes to create a diorama for your novel.

❒ Create a bulletin board display for one of the characters in your novel. Your display should share at least three important quotes about the character.

Dinner

❒ Consider all of the reasons your classmates might enjoy reading your novel. Create an advertisement using these reasons. Make it unique and interesting!

❒ Your book has been nominated for the Best Fiction Book Award. Create a trophy for this award. Include a card that describes your book and why it deserves the honor.

❒ Free choice—Submit a free-choice proposal about promoting your book to your teacher for approval.

Dessert

❒ Choose a character other than the main character who you feel was important to the novel. Design a You Be the Person presentation in which you come to class as your character and talk about your impact on the plot and theme of your novel.

❒ There are various reasons why people choose to read novels. Create a persuasive commercial that shares all of the reasons why a reader might select your novel.

Name:______________________________ Date:______________

Novel Study

Directions: Check the boxes you plan to complete. They should form a tic-tac-toe across or down. All products are due by: ______________________.

☐ *Character Analysis* Choose a character other than the main character who you feel was important to the novel. Design a You Be the Person presentation in which you come to class as your character and talk about your impact on the plot and theme of your novel.	☐ *Promoting Your Novel* Consider all of the reasons your classmates might enjoy reading your novel. Create an advertisement to encourage your classmates to read your novel. Make it unique and interesting!	☐ *Proving Your Point* Complete this statement with just one word: Everyone thinks the main character of my novel is __________. Create a cube using the six best quotes from your novel that prove your statement is true.
☐ *Proving Your Point* Determine the theme of your novel. Choose at least three quotes from your novel that strongly support the theme and at least four quotes that neither support nor disprove it. Create a folded quiz book that asks users to determine if the quotes support the theme.	☐ **Free Choice: Character Analysis** (Fill out your proposal form before beginning the free choice!)	☐ *Promoting Your Novel* There are various reasons why people choose to read novels. Create a persuasive commercial that shares all of the reasons why a reader might select your novel.
☐ *Promoting Your Novel* The Book Hall of Fame is taking nominations for the best fiction book ever written. Create a nomination video for your book. Describe your book and why it deserves the honor.	☐ *Proving Your Point* Create a bulletin board display for one of the characters in your book. Your display should share at least five important quotes about the character.	☐ *Character Analysis* Create a three-dimensional timeline for the main character in your novel. Include at least one date before the novel begins.

Novel Study Cube

Determine the best adjective to complete the following sentence: "Everyone thinks my main character is _____________." Place a quote from the story on each side of the cube to support the word you chose.

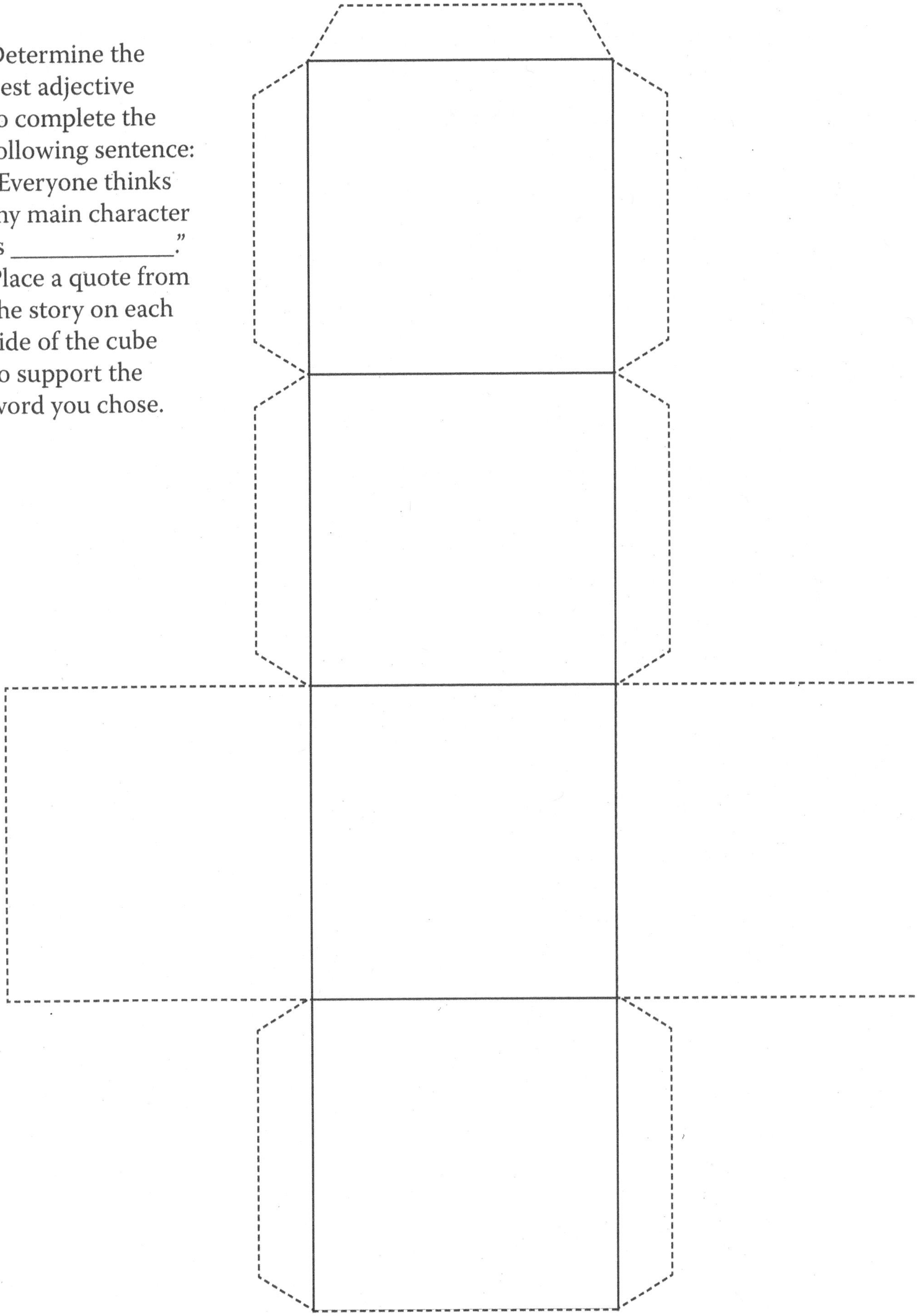

Fantasy

20-50-80 Menus

Background Information

All fantasy novels have similar elements. They usually include:

- magical creatures or beings that do not actually exist,
- an imaginary world,
- events that could not happen in real life, and
- a setting that is usually in the past.

Reading Objectives Covered Through These Menus and These Activities

- Students will make and explain inferences based on a written work.
- Students will show comprehension by retelling or acting out events in a story.
- Students will show comprehension by summarizing a story.
- Students will analyze characters, their relationships, and their importance in the story.

Writing Objectives Covered Through These Menus and These Activities

- Students will write to express their feelings, develop ideas, reflect, or problem solve.
- Students will write to influence or persuade.
- Students will exhibit voice in their writing.

Materials Needed by Students for Completion

- Socks (for puppets) ●
- Paper bags (for puppets) ●
- Story map template
- Materials for board games (e.g., folders, colored cards)
- Materials for three-dimensional timelines
- Materials for museum exhibits (e.g., boxes, cards)
- Blank index cards (for trading cards and mobiles) ▲
- Coat hangers (for mobiles) ▲
- String (for mobiles) ▲
- Materials for character models ▲

Time Frame

- 1–2 weeks—Students are given the menus as the unit is started, and the teacher discusses all of the product options on the menus. As the different options are discussed, students will choose products that add to a total of 100 points. As the lessons progress, the teacher and students refer back to the menu options associated with the content being taught.
- 1–2 days—The teacher chooses an activity or product from the menu to use with the entire class.

Suggested Forms

- All-purpose rubric
- Oral presentation rubric
- Student feedback rubric
- Free-choice proposal form

Name:______________________________ Date:______________

Fantasy

Directions: Choose at least two activities from the menu below. The activities must total at least 100 points. Place a check mark next to each box to show which activities you will complete. All activities must be completed by: ______________.

20 Points

- ❒ Create a mobile to compare and contrast our world with the world in your story or novel.
- ❒ Create a set of trading cards for all of the characters in your story or novel. Be sure to include a quote about each character on his or her card.

50 Points

- ❒ Choose a character from your story or novel and create a model of that character out of recycled materials.
- ❒ Create a board game in which players experience what your characters experience in your story or novel.
- ❒ Complete a story map for your story or novel.
- ❒ Design a three-dimensional timeline for the events in your story or novel.

80 Points

- ❒ A new museum is opening in the world of your story or novel. Based on what you know about the setting, create a museum exhibit that might be included in this new museum. Be creative!
- ❒ Free choice—Prepare a proposal form and submit your idea for approval.

Name:____________________________________ Date:____________________

Fantasy

Directions: Choose at least two activities from the menu below. The activities must total at least 100 points. Place a check mark next to each box to show which activities you will complete. All activities must be completed by: ________________________.

20 Points

- ❒ Create a Venn diagram to compare and contrast our world with the world in your story or novel.
- ❒ Complete a story map for your story or novel.

50 Points

- ❒ Choose a character from your story or novel and create a puppet of that character.
- ❒ Create a board game in which players experience what your characters experience in your story or novel.
- ❒ Design a three-dimensional timeline for the events in your story or novel. Include at least two events that could take place after the ending.
- ❒ Free choice—Prepare a proposal form and submit your idea for approval.

80 Points

- ❒ A new museum is opening in the world of your story or novel. Based on what you know about the setting, create a museum exhibit that might be included in this new museum. Be creative!
- ❒ Prepare a You Be the Person presentation in which you come to class as one of the characters from your story or novel. Be prepared to talk about how your world is different and better than ours.

Graphic Novels

List Menus

Reading Objectives Covered Through These Menus and These Activities

- Students will compare one literary work with another.
- Students will make and explain inferences based on a written work.
- Students will represent textual evidence by using story maps.
- Students will compare different forms of a written work (written versus performed).

Writing Objectives Covered Through These Menus and These Activities

- Students will write to express their feelings, develop ideas, reflect, or problem solve.
- Students will write to inform, explain, describe, or narrate.
- Students will write to influence or persuade.

Materials Needed by Students for Completion

- Poster board or large white paper
- Blank index cards (for trading cards and mobiles)
- Coat hangers (for mobiles)
- String (for mobiles)
- Large lined index cards (for recipe cards)
- Internet access (for WebQuests)
- Materials for dioramas (e.g., shoe boxes, cards)
- Story map template
- DVD or VHS recorder (for educational videos and commercials)
- Materials for three-dimensional timelines

Special Notes on the Use of These Menus

These menus give students the opportunity to create a video or commercial. Although students enjoy producing their own videos, there are often difficulties obtaining the equipment and scheduling the use of the video recorder. The menus can be modified by allowing students to act out their videos and commercials (like a play), or if students have the technology, they may wish to produce a webcam or Flash version of their videos and commercials.

These menus also allow students to create a WebQuest. There are multiple versions and templates for WebQuests available on the Internet. Teachers should decide whether to specify a certain format or allow students to create one of their own choosing.

Time Frame

- 1–2 weeks—Students are given the menus as the unit is started, and guidelines and point expectations are discussed. Students will usually need to earn 100 points for 100%, although there is an opportunity for extra credit if the teacher would like to use another target number. Because these menus cover one topic in depth, the teacher will go over all of the options on the menus and have students place check marks in the boxes next to the activities they are most interested in completing. Teachers will need to set aside a few moments with each student to sign the agreement at the bottom of the page. As instruction continues, activities are completed by students and submitted for grading.
- 1–2 days—The teacher chooses an activity or product from an objective to use with the entire class during lesson time.

Suggested Forms

- All-purpose rubric
- Oral presentation rubric
- Student feedback rubric
- Point-based free-choice proposal form

Name:______________________________ Date:__________________

Graphic Novels: Side 1

Guidelines:

1. You may complete as many of the activities listed as you can within the time period.
2. You may choose any combination of activities.
3. Your goal is 100 points. You may earn up to _____ points extra credit.
4. You may be as creative as you like within the guidelines listed below.
5. You must show your plan to your teacher by __________________.
6. Activities may be turned in at any time during the working time period. They will be graded and recorded on this sheet as you continue to work, so keep it safe!

Plan to Do	Activity to Complete (Side 1: 15–25 points)	Point Value	Date Completed	Points Earned
	Create a recipe card that shares the ingredients found in graphic novels and the steps followed when writing one.	15		
	Create a set of trading cards for the characters found in your graphic novel.	15		
	Create a Venn diagram that compares and contrasts graphic novels and comic books.	20		
	Graphic novels often use onomatopoeia. Create a mobile that shows different types of onomatopoeia. Include examples from your graphic novel as well.	20		
	Research graphic novels appropriate for your grade level. Make a list recommending graphic novels to other students.	20		
	Write Three Facts and a Fib about the content of your graphic novel.	20		
	Create a journal for a day in the life of the main character in your graphic novel.	25		
	After reading an approved graphic novel of your choice, complete a story map for it.	25		
	Choose one scene from your graphic novel and make a diorama that makes the scene frozen in time. Include dialogue in the diorama.	25		
	Design a three-dimensional timeline for the events in your graphic novel.	25		
	Total number of points you are planning to earn from Side 1.	**Total points earned from Side 1:**		

Name:______________________________ Date:____________________ ▲

Graphic Novels: Side 2

Plan to Do	Activity to Complete (Side 2: 35 points and up)	Point Value	Date Completed	Points Earned
	Choose a graphic novel that is also a movie or traditional novel. Create a commercial comparing and contrasting the story and information in the two formats.	35		
	Convert your graphic novel into a children's book.	35		
	Design a WebQuest that takes questors through the world of graphic novels.	35		
	Your teacher is not convinced that there is educational value in reading graphic novels. Create an educational video about graphic novels and their use in your class.	35		
	Survey your classmates to discover what they like and dislike about graphic novels. Share your results in a poster.	40		
	Design your own graphic novel. Be sure to include all of the elements found in graphic novels.	50		
	Free choice: must be outlined on a proposal form and approved before beginning work.	10–40 points		
	Total number of points you are planning to earn from Side 1.	**Total points earned from Side 1:**		
	Total number of points you are planning to earn from Side 2.	**Total points earned from Side 2:**		
		Grand Total (/100)		

I am planning to complete ____ activities that could earn up to a total of _____ points.

Teacher's initials _______ Student's signature ______________________________

Name:______________________________ Date:______________

Graphic Novels: Side 1

Guidelines:

1. You may complete as many of the activities listed as you can within the time period.
2. You may choose any combination of activities.
3. Your goal is 100 points. You may earn up to _____ points extra credit.
4. You may be as creative as you like within the guidelines listed below.
5. You must show your plan to your teacher by _______________.
6. Activities may be turned in at any time during the working time period. They will be graded and recorded on this sheet as you continue to work, so keep it safe!

Plan to Do	Activity to Complete (Side 1: 15–25 points)	Point Value	Date Completed	Points Earned
	Create a recipe card that shares the ingredients found in graphic novels and the steps followed when writing one.	15		
	Create a set of trading cards for the characters found in your graphic novel.	15		
	Create a Venn diagram that compares and contrasts graphic novels and comic books.	15		
	Graphic novels often use onomatopoeia. Create a mobile that shows different types of onomatopoeia. Include examples from your graphic novel as well.	15		
	After reading an approved graphic novel of your choice, complete a story map for it.	20		
	Create a journal for a day in the life of the main character in your graphic novel.	20		
	Research graphic novels appropriate for your grade level. Make a list of graphic novels you recommend to other students.	20		
	Write Three Facts and a Fib about the content of your graphic novel.	20		
	Some authors of graphic novels use color to convey moods and meanings. Does the author of your graphic novel use color this way? Create a poster that shows how color makes an impact in your graphic novel.	25		
	Choose one scene from your graphic novel and make a diorama for that scene. Include dialogue in the diorama.	25		
	Design a three-dimensional timeline for the events in your graphic novel.	25		
	Total number of points you are planning to earn from Side 1.	**Total points earned from Side 1:**		

Name:______________________________________ Date:__________________

Graphic Novels: Side 2

Plan to Do	Activity to Complete (Side 2: 30 points and up)	Point Value	Date Completed	Points Earned
	Choose a graphic novel that is also a movie or traditional novel. Create a commercial comparing and contrasting the story and information given in the two formats.	30		
	Convert your graphic novel into a children's book.	30		
	Design a WebQuest that takes questors through the world of graphic novels.	35		
	Survey your classmates to discover what they like and dislike about graphic novels. Share your results in a poster.	35		
	Your teacher is not convinced there is educational value in reading graphic novels. Create an educational video about graphic novels and their use in your class.	35		
	Design your own graphic novel. Be sure to include all of the elements found in graphic novels.	45		
	Free choice: must be outlined on a proposal form and approved before beginning work.	10–40 points		
	Total number of points you are planning to earn from Side 1.	**Total points earned from Side 1:**		
	Total number of points you are planning to earn from Side 2.	**Total points earned from Side 2:**		
		Grand Total (/100)		

I am planning to complete ____ activities that could earn up to a total of _____ points.

Teacher's initials _______ Student's signature ________________________________

Historical Fiction

20-50-80 Menus

Background Information

All historical fiction novels have similar elements. They usually include:

- a combination of fact and fiction in a realistic way that takes the reader back in time,
- a historical setting with both real and fictional historical characters and events, and
- an interesting problem that may or may not be based on actual historical events.

Reading Objectives Covered Through These Menus and These Activities

- Students will make and explain inferences based on a written work.
- Students will show comprehension by retelling or acting out events in a story.
- Students will distinguish between an author's opinion and fact.

Writing Objectives Covered Through These Menus and These Activities

- Students will write to inform, explain, describe, or narrate.
- Students will write to influence or persuade.
- Students will exhibit voice in their writing.

Materials Needed by Students for Completion

- Poster board or large white paper ▲
- Internet access (for WebQuests)
- Historical story map template
- Microsoft PowerPoint or other slideshow software ●
- Materials for board games (e.g., file folders, cards)

Special Notes on the Use of These Menus

These menus allow students to create a WebQuest. There are multiple versions and templates for WebQuests available on the Internet. Teachers should decide whether to specify a certain format or allow students to create one of their own choosing.

Time Frame

- 1–2 weeks—Students are given the menus as the unit is started, and the teacher discusses all of the product options on the menus. As the different options are discussed, students will choose products that add to a total of 100 points. As the lessons progress, the teacher and students refer back to the menu options associated with the content being taught.
- 1–2 days—The teacher chooses an activity or product from the menu to use with the entire class.

Suggested Forms

- All-purpose rubric
- Oral presentation rubric
- Student feedback rubric
- Point-based free-choice proposal form

Name:____ Date:____________________ ▲

Historical Fiction

Directions: Choose at least two activities from the menu below. The activities must total at least 100 points. Place a check mark next to each box to show which activities you will complete. All activities must be completed by: ________________________.

20 Points

- ❒ Make a Venn diagram to compare and contrast your reading to what is known from history.
- ❒ Create a fact and fiction T-chart on a poster that shares what is real and what is fiction in your reading.

50 Points

- ❒ Pretend that you are a character other than the main character in your reading and keep a diary for 5 days. Include your thoughts about the other characters and their actions.
- ❒ Create a board game in which players learn about the time period of your book.
- ❒ Create a historical fiction story map for your reading.
- ❒ Free choice—Prepare a proposal form and submit your idea for approval.

80 Points

- ❒ Create a WebQuest that takes questors to various historical websites from your reading's time period. Your WebQuest should ask questions that would help questors better understand your characters and their actions.
- ❒ People sometimes consider alternate histories—what could have happened instead of actual history. Pretend that your main character made a different choice in the reading, and rewrite the ending considering this new choice.

Name:____ Date:____________________

Historical Fiction

Directions: Choose at least two activities from the menu below. The activities must total at least 100 points. Place a check mark next to each box to show which activities you will complete. All activities must be completed by: ____________________.

20 Points

- ❐ Create a historical fiction story map for your reading.
- ❐ Create a PowerPoint presentation that shares the history behind your reading.

50 Points

- ❐ Pretend that you are a character other than the main character in your reading and keep a diary for a week. Include your impressions of the other characters and their actions.
- ❐ Create a board game in which players adventure through the time period of your book.
- ❐ Create a WebQuest that takes questors to various historical websites from your reading's time period. Your WebQuest should ask questions that would help others better understand your characters and their actions.
- ❐ Free choice—Prepare a proposal form and submit your idea for approval.

80 Points

- ❐ Research important historical figures that were not mentioned in your book. Prepare a You Be the Person presentation in which you come to class as one of these people and give your opinion on the actions of one of the characters in the reading.
- ❐ People sometimes consider alternate histories—what could have happened instead of actual history. Pretend that your main character made a different choice in the reading, and rewrite the ending considering this new choice.

Name:_______________________________________ Date:____________________

Historical Story Map

Title and Author

Historical Setting

Include dates and important locations.

Real Characters From History

Include at least two traits for each character; for each trait, include a quote from the reading to provide support.

Fictional Characters From History

Include at least two traits for each character; for each trait, include a quote that provides support.

Problem

Be sure to include whether or not this problem actually happened in the past.

Major Events in the Story

Resolution

Mystery and Suspense

20-50-80 Menus

Background Information

All mystery and suspense novels have similar elements. They usually include:

- a crime or something unusual that has happened,
- a main character who is trying to solve the situation using clues,
- a possibly scary setting and suspicious characters, and
- built-in suspense so that the reader really wants to know what happens next.

Reading Objectives Covered Through These Menus and These Activities

- Students will compare one literary work with another.
- Students will make and explain inferences based on the written work.
- Students will represent textual evidence by using story maps.

Writing Objectives Covered Through These Menus and These Activities

- Students will write to express their feelings, develop ideas, reflect, or problem solve.
- Students will write to inform, explain, describe, or narrate.
- Students will write to influence or persuade.

Materials Needed by Students for Completion

- Poster board or large white paper
- Blank index cards (for trading cards) ▲
- Mystery story map template
- DVD or VHS recorder (for news reports)
- Materials for three-dimensional timelines ●
- Clue™ board game (optional)
- Magazines (for collages) ▲
- Materials for board games (e.g., file folders, cards)

Special Notes on the Use of These Menus

These menus give students the opportunity to create a news report. Although students enjoy producing their own videos, there are often difficulties obtaining the equipment and scheduling the use of the video recorder. The menus can be modified by allowing students to act out their news reports (like a play), or if students have the technology, they may wish to produce a webcam or Flash version of their news reports.

Time Frame

- 1–2 weeks—Students are given the menus as the unit is started, and the teacher discusses all of the product options on the menus. As the different options are discussed, students will choose products that add to a total of 100 points. As the lessons progress, the teacher and students refer back to the menu options associated with the content being taught.
- 1–2 days—The teacher chooses an activity or product from the menu to use with the entire class.

Suggested Forms

- All-purpose rubric
- Oral presentation rubric
- Student feedback rubric
- Point-based free-choice proposal form

Name:______________________________ Date:____________________

Mystery and Suspense

Directions: Choose at least two activities from the menu below. The activities must total at least 100 points. Place a check mark next to each box to show which activities you will complete. All activities must be completed by: ____________________.

20 Points

- ❒ Create a set of trading cards for all of the characters who are involved in the mystery. They may be the characters investigating the mystery or your suspects. Indicate their roles on the cards.
- ❒ Create a collage of pictures that could represent the characters and events in your story or novel.

50 Points

- ❒ The game Clue™ is a mystery board game. Create your own mystery board game based on the story or novel that you have read.
- ❒ Complete the mystery story map for your story or novel.
- ❒ Write a newspaper article that may have been written about the mystery or crime committed in your story or novel.
- ❒ Free choice—Prepare a proposal form and submit your idea for approval.

80 Points

- ❒ Using the mystery story map to brainstorm, create and write your own mystery or suspense story.
- ❒ Create a news report covering the mystery or crime committed in your story or novel. Pretend that you are on the scene right after the crime has happened and share your thoughts on the suspect(s).

Name:____ Date:______________________

Mystery and Suspense

Directions: Choose at least two activities from the menu below. The activities must total at least 100 points. Place a check mark next to each box to show which activities you will complete. All activities must be completed by: ________________________.

20 Points

- ❒ Create a three-dimensional timeline of clues or information found in your story or novel.
- ❒ Complete the mystery story map for your story or novel.

50 Points

- ❒ The game Clue™ is a mystery board game. Create your own mystery board game based on the story or novel you have read.
- ❒ Create a news report covering the mystery or crime committed in your story or novel. Pretend that you are on the scene right after the crime has happened and share your thoughts on the suspect(s).
- ❒ Find a school-appropriate song that involves a mystery and create a Venn diagram to compare and contrast the song with your story or novel.
- ❒ Free choice—Prepare a proposal form and submit your idea for approval.

80 Points

- ❒ Using the mystery story map to brainstorm, create and write your own mystery or suspense story.
- ❒ Choose the most important scenes and clues from your mystery story or novel and turn them into a play. When you perform your play, the audience should be trying to solve the mystery based on the information you provide in the play.

Name:_______________________________ Date:_______________

Mystery or Suspense Story Map

Title and Author

Setting

Main Characters

Write at least three traits for each main character.

Suspicious Characters

Record information about each suspicious character showing what makes him or her suspicious.

Mystery, Crime, or Problem to Be Solved

Major Events or Clues

Include the character who found the information and how it was discovered.

Explanation of the Mystery or Crime

Bring all of the clues together!

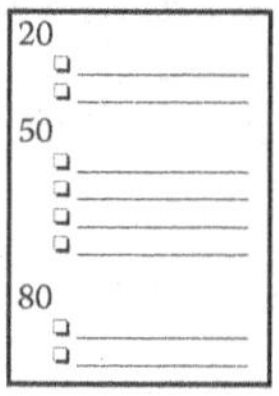

Mythology

20-50-80 Menus

Background Information

Long ago, people made up stories to explain things they didn't understand. Many believed that there were gods and goddesses who caused things to happen. People also made up stories of heroes who faced great challenges and interacted with these gods. All myths have similar elements. They usually include:

- a setting in the ancient past,
- gods or goddesses who affect what happens to people,
- a story explaining how or why something happened, and
- a moral or lesson.

Reading Objectives Covered Through These Menus and These Activities

- Students will make and explain inferences based on a written work.
- Students will show comprehension by retelling or acting out events in a story.
- Students will show comprehension by summarizing information.

Writing Objectives Covered Through These Menus and These Activities

- Students will write to inform, explain, describe, or narrate.
- Students will exhibit voice in their writing.

Materials Needed by Students for Completion

- Poster board or large white paper
- Blank index cards (for trading cards)
- Socks (for puppets) ▲
- Paper bags (for puppets) ▲
- Materials for dioramas (e.g., shoe boxes, cards) ●

Time Frame

- 1–2 weeks—Students are given the menus as the unit is started, and the teacher discusses all of the product options on the menus. As the different options are discussed, students will choose products that add to a total of 100 points. As the lessons progress, the teacher and

students refer back to the menu options associated with the content being taught.
- 1–2 days—The teacher chooses an activity or product from the menu to use with the entire class.

Suggested Forms
- All-purpose rubric
- Oral presentation rubric
- Student feedback form
- Point-based free-choice proposal form

Name:______________________________ Date:______________________

Mythology

Directions: Choose at least two activities from the menu below. The activities must total at least 100 points. Place a check mark next to each box to show which activities you will complete. All activities must be completed by: ______________________.

20 Points

- ❒ Create a set of trading cards for the gods, goddesses, and important characters mentioned in your reading.
- ❒ Create a windowpane that shows all of the elements of a good myth.

50 Points

- ❒ Create Three Facts and a Fib about a character in the myth that you read.
- ❒ Create a puppet for one of the characters from your reading. Your puppet should be ready to talk about what he or she learned.
- ❒ Read another myth with a different god or goddess in it. Create a Venn diagram to compare and contrast the two gods or goddesses.
- ❒ Free choice—Prepare a proposal form and submit your idea for approval.

80 Points

- ❒ Write a modern-day myth to explain something mysterious from the present day.
- ❒ Most gods and goddesses have special skills or interests. Create an advertisement for your deity showcasing his or her special skills or interests.

Name:____ Date:_____________________

Mythology

Directions: Choose at least two activities from the menu below. The activities must total at least 100 points. Place a check mark next to each box to show which activities you will complete. All activities must be completed by: ____________________.

20 Points

- ❒ Create Three Facts and a Fib about a character in your reading.
- ❒ Create a set of trading cards for the gods, goddesses, and important characters mentioned in your reading.

50 Points

- ❒ Read another myth that has the same god or goddess in it. Create a Venn diagram to compare and contrast this character's personality in the two myths. Include quotes from each myth in your diagram.
- ❒ Create a diorama and include one of the characters from your reading. Your diorama should show your character and his or her setting.
- ❒ Most gods and goddesses have special skills or interests. Pretend that you could speak to one of the gods or goddesses in your reading. Create and complete an interview with your deity about his or her special skills or interests.
- ❒ Free choice—Prepare a proposal form and submit your idea for approval.

80 Points

- ❒ Write a modern-day myth to explain something mysterious from the present day.
- ❒ Convert your reading into a play, but provide a different ending that makes sense based on the message of the reading.

Plays

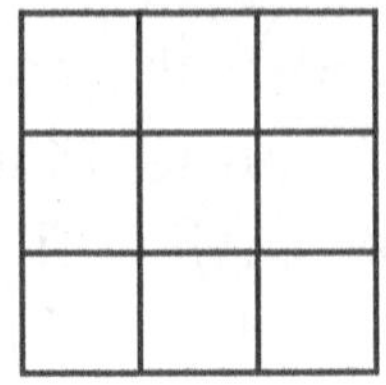

Meal Menu ▲ and Tic-Tac-Toe Menu ●

Reading Objectives Covered Through These Menus and These Activities

- Students will show comprehension by retelling or acting out events in a story.
- Students will compare different forms of a written work (written versus performed).
- Students will compare one literary genre with another.

Writing Objectives Covered Through These Menus and These Activities

- Students will write to express their feelings, develop ideas, reflect, or problem solve.
- Students will exhibit voice in their writing.
- Students will use vivid language.

Materials Needed by Students for Completion

- Poster board or large white paper
- Socks (for puppets)
- Paper bags (for puppets)
- Large lined index cards (for recipe cards)
- Materials for board games (e.g., folders, colored cards) ▲
- DVD or VHS recorder (for commercials) ●

Special Notes on the Use of These Menus

This topic has two different menu formats: Meal menu and Tic-Tac-Toe menu. The Meal menu is specifically selected for its meal-oriented, Bloom's-based options, as it is easily broken into manageable bits. The menu can be cut into strips, each strip featuring its own meal, to be given to students. This way, once students have chosen and submitted the breakfast product for grading, they can move on to the lunch strip, and lastly, they can complete the dinner and dessert strips. Because this type of menu is designed to become more advanced as students move through the meals, teachers may choose to provide their students who have special needs with just the meals and save the dessert for enrichment.

These menus are set up so that each student will be creating his or her own play. Making time for all of these presentations may seem daunting;

teachers have several options for making enough time for all of the students to perform. Students can be put into small groups of two or three if they have chosen the same option on their menus. As another option, students can work on their own product and then have others play roles in their productions. Lastly, if time is a consideration, it is definitely a good idea to have students record their productions for sharing at a later, more convenient time.

Time Frame

- 2–3 weeks—Students are given the menus as the unit is started. As the teacher presents lessons throughout the week, he or she should refer back to the menu options associated with that content. The teacher will go over all of the options for that content and have students place check marks in the boxes that represent the activities they are most interested in completing. If students are using the Tic-Tac-Toe menu form, activities chosen and completed should make a column or row. If students are using the Meal menu form, students will complete one product from each meal, with dessert being an optional enrichment product. When students complete these patterns, they will have completed one activity from each content area, learning style, or level of Bloom's Revised taxonomy.
- 1 week—At the start of the unit, the teacher chooses the three activities he or she feels are most valuable for students. Stations can be set up in the classroom. These three activities are available for student choice throughout the week as regular instruction takes place.
- 1–2 days—The teacher chooses an activity from the menu to use with the entire class.

Suggested Forms

- All-purpose rubric
- Oral presentation rubric
- Student feedback rubric
- Free-choice proposal form

Name:______________________________ Date:______________________

Plays

Directions: Choose one activity each for breakfast, lunch, and dinner. Dessert is an activity you can choose to do after you have finished your other meals. All products must be completed by: ________________.

Breakfast

- ❒ After choosing a play that you have both read and seen performed (either live, as a film, or on TV), write Three Facts and a Fib that compare and contrast your written play to the one that was performed.
- ❒ Choose a play that you have seen performed either on television or in person. Design a windowpane that compares and contrasts the two performances.
- ❒ Create a board game version of your play. Write a paragraph that shares the main differences between the events of the play and the events in your board game.

Lunch

- ❒ Create an advertisement to promote your play. Be sure to include the aspects of your play that you found most interesting to persuade others to read it.
- ❒ Create a recipe card for an excellent play, and then compare the play you read with your card and write a paragraph about your play.
- ❒ Free choice—Submit a proposal about your play to your teacher for approval.

Dinner

- ❒ Choose one of your favorite fictional stories. Convert this story into a play.
- ❒ Make an original puppet show with at least two characters to share with your classmates.
- ❒ Turn your favorite nursery rhyme into a play. Give it a new ending!

Dessert

- ❒ After reading a play, convert it into children's book. Design a book cover for your book. Include comments that explain how the play and the children's book are similar and different.
- ❒ Read a play of your choice. Write a newspaper review that expresses your thoughts about the quality of the play and why you feel this way.

Name:______________________________ Date:______________________

Plays

Directions: Check the boxes you plan to complete. They should form a tic-tac-toe across or down. All products are due by: ______________________.

☐ *Evaluating Your Play* Create a commercial to promote your play. Be sure to include the aspects of your play that you found most interesting to persuade others to read it.	☐ *Create Your Own Play* Choose one of your favorite fictional stories. Convert this story into a play.	☐ *Compare Your Play* Choose a play that you have seen performed either on television or in person. Design a mind map that compares and contrasts the two performances.
☐ *Compare Your Play* After reading a play, convert it into a children's book. Design a book cover for your book. Include comments that explain how the play and the children's book are similar and different.	☐ **Free Choice: Evaluating Your Play** (Fill out your proposal form before beginning the free choice!)	☐ *Create Your Own Play* Make an original puppet show with at least two characters to share with your classmates.
☐ *Create Your Own Play* Plays are more than just lines being said. Create a play that depends on stage directions or character actions and uses no more than two words during the entire production.	☐ *Compare Your Play* After choosing a play that you have both read and seen performed (either live, as a film, or on TV), write Three Facts and a Fib that compare and contrast your written play to the one that was performed.	☐ *Evaluating Your Play* Create a recipe card for an excellent play, and then compare the play you read with your card and write a paragraph evaluating your play.

Poetry

List Menus

Reading Objectives Covered Through These Menus and These Activities

- Students will interpret figurative language and multiple-meaning words.
- Students will use resources and references to build meaning.

Writing Objectives Covered Through These Menus and These Activities

- Students will write to express their feelings, develop ideas, and reflect.
- Students will write to inform, explain, describe, or narrate.
- Students will use vivid language.

Materials Needed by Students for Completion

- Poster board or large white paper
- Internet access (for WebQuests)
- Materials for bulletin board displays
- Coat hangers (for mobiles)
- Blank index cards (for mobiles)
- String (for mobiles)
- Microsoft PowerPoint or other slideshow software
- Newspapers
- Blank index cards (for concentration cards)
- Shel Silverstein poetry books

Special Notes on the Use of These Menus

These menus allow students to create a bulletin board display. Some classrooms may only have one bulletin board, so the teacher can divide the board into sections, or additional classroom wall or hall space can be sectioned off for the creation of these displays. Students can plan their displays based on the amount of space they are assigned.

These menus also allow students to create a WebQuest. There are multiple versions and templates for WebQuests available on the Internet. Teachers should decide whether to specify a certain format or allow students to create one of their own choosing.

Time Frame

- 1–2 weeks—Students are given the menus as the unit is started, and guidelines and point expectations are discussed. Students will usually need to earn 100 points for 100%, although there is an opportunity for extra credit if the teacher would like to use another target number. Because these menus cover one topic in depth, the teacher will go over all of the options on the menus and have students place check marks in the boxes next to the activities they are most interested in completing. Teachers will need to set aside a few moments with each student to sign the agreement at the bottom of the page. As instruction continues, activities are completed by students and submitted for grading.
- 1–2 days—The teacher chooses an activity or product from an objective to use with the entire class during lesson time.

Suggested Forms

- All-purpose rubric
- Oral presentation rubric
- Student feedback rubric
- Point-based free-choice proposal form

Name:______________________________ Date:________________

Poetry: Side 1

Guidelines:

1. You may complete as many of the activities listed as you can within the time period.
2. You may choose any combination of activities.
3. Your goal is 100 points. You may earn up to _____ points extra credit.
4. You may be as creative as you like within the guidelines listed below.
5. You must show your plan to your teacher by ________________.
6. Activities may be turned in at any time during the working time period. They will be graded and recorded on this sheet as you continue to work, so keep it safe!

Plan to Do	Activity to Complete (Side 1: 15–30 points)	Point Value	Date Completed	Points Earned
	Create a mind map of rhyming words that could be used when writing a poem.	15		
	Select a longer poem and create a set of concentration cards in which players match the beginning of a stanza with its ending.	15		
	After choosing your favorite book of poetry, design a book cover for it.	20		
	Create a book of poetry with examples from at least three different poetry types (e.g., diamante, haiku, name poem, free verse).	20		
	Research the history of the haiku. Make a poster that shows your research as well as two examples of this type of poem.	20		
	Create a mobile that shares different ways that poems are used in our daily lives (in addition to books of poetry).	20		
	Choose a poem from one of Shel Silverstein's poetry books. Create your own drawing or illustration for the poem.	25		
	Create a mural based on a scene described in a poem.	25		
	Choose one of your favorite poems and transform it into a song or rap. Share your song or rap with the class.	25		
	Create a brochure about poetry, the different types of poems, and the various reasons people write poems.	30		
	Total number of points you are planning to earn from Side 1.		**Total points earned from Side 1:**	

Name:____ Date:____________________ ▲

Poetry: Side 2

Plan to Do	Activity to Complete (Side 2: 35 points and up)	Point Value	Date Completed	Points Earned
	Research poems that have been banned for cultural reasons. Choose one and create a PowerPoint presentation about the poem. Explain why it was banned and give your opinion on the issue.	35		
	Create a bulletin board display that shows how poetry can affect its readers. Include examples of various poems.	35		
	Write and perform a play that includes two original poems you wrote.	35		
	Create your own children's book of poetry with at least three poems you have written.	40		
	Design a WebQuest that takes questors through various examples of poetry, both old and new, allowing them to read and evaluate the poems.	40		
	Select a newspaper article about a current event. Using the information in the article, create and recite a poem about the event.	40		
	Free choice: must be outlined on a proposal form and approved before beginning work.	10–40 points		
	Total number of points you are planning to earn from Side 1.		**Total points earned from Side 1:**	
	Total number of points you are planning to earn from Side 2.		**Total points earned from Side 2:**	
			Grand Total (/100)	

I am planning to complete ____ activities that could earn up to a total of _____ points.

Teacher's initials _______ Student's signature ______________________________

Name:____ Date:______________________

Poetry: Side 1

Guidelines:

1. You may complete as many of the activities listed as you can within the time period.
2. You may choose any combination of activities.
3. Your goal is 100 points. You may earn up to _____ points extra credit.
4. You may be as creative as you like within the guidelines listed below.
5. You must show your plan to your teacher by ________________.
6. Activities may be turned in at any time during the working time period. They will be graded and recorded on this sheet as you continue to work, so keep it safe!

Plan to Do	Activity to Complete (Side 1: 15–25 points)	Point Value	Date Completed	Points Earned
	Create a mind map of rhyming words that could be used when writing a poem.	15		
	Create a book of poetry with examples from at least three different poetry types (e.g., diamante, haiku, name poem, free verse).	15		
	Research the history of the haiku. Make a poster that shows your research as well as three examples of this type of poem.	15		
	Create a mobile that shares all of the different ways that poems are used in our daily lives (in addition to books of poetry).	15		
	Select a longer poem and create a set of concentration cards in which players match the beginning of a stanza with its ending.	15		
	After choosing your favorite book of poetry, design a book cover for it.	20		
	Choose a poem from one of Shel Silverstein's poetry books. Create your own drawing or illustration for the poem you choose.	20		
	Choose one of your favorite poems and transform it into a song or rap. Share your song or rap with your class.	20		
	Create a mural based on a scene described in a poem.	20		
	Create a brochure about poetry, the different types of poems, and the various reasons people write poetry.	25		
	Total number of points you are planning to earn from Side 1.		**Total points earned from Side 1:**	

Name:_______________________ Date:_______________

Poetry: Side 2

Plan to Do	Activity to Complete (Side 2: 30 points and up)	Point Value	Date Completed	Points Earned
	Create a bulletin board display that shows the impact poetry can have on its readers. Include examples of various poems.	30		
	Research poems that have been banned for cultural reasons. Choose one and create a PowerPoint presentation about the poem. Explain why it was banned and give your opinion on the issue.	30		
	Write and perform a play featuring two original poems you wrote.	30		
	Create your own children's book of poetry with at least five poems you have written.	35		
	Design a WebQuest that takes questors through various examples of poetry, both old and new, allowing them to read and evaluate the poems.	35		
	Select a newspaper article about a current event. Using the information in the article, create and recite a poem about the event.	35		
	Free choice: must be outlined on a proposal form and approved before beginning work.	10–40 points		
	Total number of points you are planning to earn from Side 1.	**Total points earned from Side 1:**		
	Total number of points you are planning to earn from Side 2.	**Total points earned from Side 2:**		
		Grand Total (/100)		

I am planning to complete _____ activities that could earn up to a total of _____ points.

Teacher's initials _______ Student's signature ______________________

Science Fiction

Meal Menu ▲ and Tic-Tac-Toe Menu ●

Background Information

All science fiction novels have similar elements. Science fiction works usually include:

- futuristic settings or settings on another planet;
- events that could not happen in today's world;
- a story or theme that is based upon science or technology, often exploring what is possible; and
- themes including alternate worlds, time travel, cloning, and the end of the world as we know it.

Reading Objectives Covered Through These Menus and These Activities

- Students will make and explain inferences based on a written work.
- Students will show comprehension by retelling or acting out events in a story.
- Students will analyze characters, their relationships, and their importance in the story.

Writing Objectives Covered Through These Menus and These Activities

- Students will write to express their feelings, develop ideas, reflect, or problem solve.
- Students will exhibit voice in their writing.

Materials Needed by Students for Completion

- Coat hangers (for mobiles)
- Blank index cards (for mobiles and trading cards ▲)
- String (for mobiles)
- Rulers (for comic strips)
- DVD or VHS recorder (for commercials and news reports)
- Materials for board games (e.g., folders, colored cards)
- Story map template
- Materials for three-dimensional timelines ▲

Special Notes on the Use of These Menus

This topic has two different menu formats: Meal menu and Tic-Tac-Toe menu. The Meal menu is specifically selected for its meal-oriented,

Bloom's-based options, as it is easily broken into manageable bits. The menu can be cut into strips, each strip featuring its own meal, to be given to students. This way, once students have chosen and submitted the breakfast product for grading, they can move on to the lunch strip, and lastly, they can complete the dinner and dessert strips. Because this type of menu is designed to become more advanced as students move through the meals, teachers may choose to provide their students who have special needs with just the meals and save the dessert for enrichment.

These menus also give students the opportunity to create a commercial or news report. Although students enjoy producing their own videos, there are often difficulties obtaining the equipment and scheduling the use of the video recorder. The menus can be modified by allowing students to act out their commercials and news reports (like a play), or if students have the technology, they may wish to produce a webcam or Flash version of their commercials and news reports.

Time Frame

- 2–3 weeks—Students are given the menus as the unit is started. As the teacher presents lessons throughout the week, he or she should refer back to the menu options associated with that content. The teacher will go over all of the options for that content and have students place check marks in the boxes that represent the activities they are most interested in completing. If students are using the Tic-Tac-Toe menu form, activities chosen and completed should make a column or row. If students are using the Meal menu form, students will complete one product from each meal, with dessert being an optional enrichment product. When students complete these patterns, they will have completed one activity from each content area, learning style, or level of Bloom's Revised taxonomy.
- 1 week—At the start of the unit, the teacher chooses the three activities he or she feels are most valuable for students. Stations can be set up in the classroom. These three activities are available for student choice throughout the week as regular instruction takes place.
- 1–2 days—The teacher chooses an activity from the menu to use with the entire class.

Suggested Forms

- All-purpose rubric
- Oral presentation rubric
- Student feedback rubric
- Free-choice proposal form

Name:____________________________________ Date:__________________ ▲

Science Fiction

Directions: Choose one activity each for breakfast, lunch, and dinner. Dessert is an activity you can choose to do after you have finished your other meals. All products must be completed by: __________________.

Breakfast

❒ Create a set of trading cards for all of the characters in your reading selection. Be sure to include all of the characters, whether they are human or not!

❒ Consider the elements necessary for a written work to be considered science fiction. Create a mobile that shows examples of these elements in your reading.

❒ Complete a story map for your science fiction reading. Include the aspects of the plot that let you know that what you're reading is science fiction.

Lunch

❒ Create an advertisement for an item or invention used in your reading selection that does not exist in our time or has been changed significantly.

❒ Create a brochure to convince people to travel to or visit the location in your reading selection. Be persuasive!

❒ Free choice—Submit a proposal for your science fiction selection to your teacher for approval.

Dinner

❒ After reading your science fiction selection, create a board game with the same theme. Be sure that your board game incorporates quotes about your characters as well as their impact on the plot.

❒ After reading your science fiction selection, identify the most important events and create a three-dimensional timeline of the events.

❒ Identify your favorite science fiction character and show his or her next adventure using a comic strip format. Be creative; include a new setting and adventure for your character.

Dessert

❒ Science fiction novels are often filled with lots of drama or action. Create a news report that documents the most important event in your science fiction selection.

❒ Write your own science fiction story set in the future. Include a story map that shows your prewriting as well as your rough draft.

Name:______________________________ Date:__________________

Science Fiction

Directions: Check the boxes you plan to complete. They should form a tic-tac-toe across or down. All products are due by: ________________________.

☐ *Share It*	☐ *Live It*	☐ *Make It Mobile*
After reading your science fiction work, identify the most important ideas and rewrite your work as a children's book.	Choose the scene from your science fiction work that you feel had the greatest impact on the plot. Reenact this scene from the piece in a play.	Consider the elements necessary for a written work to be considered science fiction. Create a mobile that shows examples of these elements in your reading.
☐ *Draw It* Identify your favorite science fiction character and depict his or her next adventure using a cartoon format. Be creative; include a new setting and adventure for your character.	☐ **Free Choice: Science Fiction** (Fill out your proposal form before beginning the free choice!)	☐ *Advertise It* Create a commercial for an item or invention used in your reading selection that does not exist in our time or has been changed significantly.
☐ *Document It* Science fiction novels are often filled with lots of drama or action. Create a news report that documents the most important event in your reading selection.	☐ *Play With It* After reading your science fiction work, create a board game with the same theme. Be sure that your board game incorporates quotes about your characters as well as their impact on the plot.	☐ *Write It* Write your own science fiction story set in the future. Include a story map that shows your prewriting as well as your rough draft.

Chapter 6

Writing and Mechanics

DOI: 10.4324/9781003234227-7

Parts of Speech

Game Show Menus

Reading Objectives Covered Through These Menus and These Activities

- Students will give examples of various parts of speech encountered in readings.
- Students will use resources and references to build meaning.

Writing Objectives Covered Through These Menus and These Activities

- Students will write to inform, explain, describe, or narrate.
- Students will exhibit voice in their writing.
- Students will use vivid language.

Materials Needed by Students for Completion

- Poster board or large white paper
- Coat hangers (for mobiles)
- Blank index cards (for mobiles and trading cards)
- String (for mobiles)
- Dictionary
- Scrapbooking materials
- Magazines (for collages)
- Materials for board games (e.g., folders, colored cards)
- Large lined index cards (for instruction cards)
- Materials for bulletin board displays
- Materials for trophies ▲
- Materials for quiz boards (e.g., batteries, holiday lights, aluminum foil, tape)
- Microsoft PowerPoint or other slideshow software ▲
- Materials for class games ●

Special Notes on the Use of These Menus

These menus allow students to create a bulletin board display. Some classrooms may only have one bulletin board, so the teacher can divide the board into sections, or additional classroom wall or hall space can be sectioned off for the creation of these displays. Students can plan their displays based on the amount of space they are assigned.

These menus also offer students the opportunity to create a quiz board. Quiz boards can range from simple to very complex, depending on the knowledge and ability of the student. Quiz boards work best when the teacher creates a "tester" that can be used to check any boards that are submitted. Basic instructions on how to create quiz boards and testers can be found at http://www.cesiscience.org/attachments/article/100/QuizBoardDirections.pdf.

The circle menu gives students the opportunity to create a class game. The length of the game is not stated in the product guidelines, so the teacher can determine what works best. It may be a good idea to have students start with shorter games and work up to longer games with a review focus.

Time Frame

- 2–3 weeks—Students are given the menus as the unit is started, and the guidelines and point expectations are discussed. As lessons are taught throughout the unit, students and the teacher can refer back to the options associated with the topic. The teacher will go over all of the options for the topic being covered and will have students place check marks in the boxes next to the activities they are most interested in completing. As teaching continues throughout the 2–3 weeks, activities are discussed, chosen, and submitted for grading.
- 1 week—At the beginning of the unit, the teacher chooses an activity from each area that he or she feels would be most valuable for students. Stations can be set up in the classroom. These activities are available for student choice throughout the week as regular instruction takes place.
- 1–2 days—The teacher chooses an activity from an objective to use with the entire class during lesson time.

Suggested Forms

- All-purpose rubric
- Oral presentation rubric
- Oral presentation feedback form
- Free-choice proposal form for point-based products

Name:____ Date:______________________

Guidelines for the Parts of Speech Game Show Menu

- You must choose at least one activity from each topic area.
- You may not do more than two activities in any one topic area for credit. (You are, of course, welcome to do more than two for your own investigation.)
- Grading will be ongoing, so turn in products as you complete them.
- All free-choice proposals must be turned in and approved prior to working on that free-choice product.
- You must earn 100 points for a 100%. You may earn extra credit up to _____ points.
- You must show your teacher your plan for completion by: _________.

Name:______________________________ Date:__________________

Parts of Speech

Nouns	Adjectives	Verbs	Adverbs	Prepositions	Points for Each Level
❒ Design a flipbook for the different types of nouns. Include at least three examples of each type. (10 pts.)	❒ Make a mobile with at least 15 words that could replace the adjective "good" in the following sentence, yet not change the meaning: They were good students. (15 pts.)	❒ Create a collage of pictures that represent verbs. List each verb on the back of the collage. (15 pts.)	❒ Make an instruction card that shows how to change adjectives into adverbs. (15 pts.)	❒ Make a preposition mind map that classifies all of the prepositions. (10 pts.)	**10–15 points**
❒ Create a song or rap to teach your classmates about the different types of nouns we use on a daily basis. (20 pts.)	❒ Using a dictionary, select five adjectives that you do not already know. Create trading cards for the words to help you and your classmates learn them. (20 pts.)	❒ Create a board game that allows players to practice identifying and using the different types of verbs. (25 pts.)	❒ Design a bulletin board display to teach how to use adverbs in written works. (25 pts.)	❒ Choose a story and analyze all of the prepositions that are used in the story. Which seems most important? Create a trophy that shows this proposition's importance. (25 pts.)	**20–25 points**
❒ Create a children's ABC book with nouns that are meaningful to others your age. There will be 26 words in all, one for each letter of the alphabet. (30 pts.)	❒ Design your personal scrapbook with pages devoted to at least six different adjectives that describe you. (30 pts.)	❒ Keep a verb diary for one hour in which you record every verb you hear or say. Then sort the verbs based on their types. (30 pts.)	❒ The verb told the adverb that it was not an important part of speech. The adverb disagreed. Create a PowerPoint of examples that prove the adverb is important. (30 pts.)	❒ Create a quiz board that quizzes users on identifying prepositional phrases found in popular songs. (30 pts.)	**30 points**
Free Choice (prior approval) (25–50 pts.)	**Free Choice** (prior approval) (25–50 pts.)	**Free Choice** (prior approval) (25–50 pts.)	**Free Choice** (prior approval) (25–50 pts.)	**Free Choice** (prior approval) (25–50 pts.)	**25–50 points**
Total:	**Total:**	**Total:**	**Total:**	**Total:**	**Total Grade:**

Name:______________________ Date:______________

Parts of Speech

Nouns	Adjectives	Verbs	Adverbs	Prepositions	Points for Each Level
❒ Design a flipbook for the different types of nouns. Include at least five examples of each type. (10 pts.)	❒ Make a mobile with at least 20 words that could replace the adjective "good" in the following sentence, yet not change the meaning: They were good students. (15 pts.)	❒ Create a collage of pictures that represent verbs. List each verb on the back of the collage. (10 pts.)	❒ Make an instruction card that shows how to change adjectives into adverbs. (10 pts.)	❒ Make a preposition mind map that classifies all of the prepositions. (10 pts.)	**10–15 points**
❒ Create Three Facts and a Fib about identifying different types of nouns. (20 pts.)	❒ Using a dictionary, select 10 adjectives that you do not already know. Create trading cards for the words to help you and your classmates learn them. (20 pts.)	❒ Create a board game that allows players to practice identifying and using the different types of verbs. (20 pts.)	❒ Design a bulletin board display to teach how to use adverbs in written works. (20 pts.)	❒ Create a quiz board that quizzes users on identifying prepositional phrases found in popular songs. (20 pts.)	**20 points**
❒ Create a children's ABC book with nouns that are meaningful to others your age. There will be 26 words in all, one for each letter of the alphabet. (30 pts.)	❒ Design your personal scrapbook with pages devoted to at least six different adjectives that describe you. (30 pts.)	❒ You have been named the director of a new game show called "Name That Verb." Create and perform your game show. (30 pts.)	❒ The verb told the adverb that it was not an important part of speech. The adverb disagreed. Create a speech that the adverb could give to prove that it is very important. (30 pts.)	❒ Create a class game to practice recognizing and using prepositions properly. (30 pts.)	**30 points**
Free Choice (prior approval) (25–50 pts.)	**Free Choice** (prior approval) (25–50 pts.)	**Free Choice** (prior approval) (25–50 pts.)	**Free Choice** (prior approval) (25–50 pts.)	**Free Choice** (prior approval) (25–50 pts.)	**25–50 points**
Total:	**Total:**	**Total:**	**Total:**	**Total:**	**Total Grade:**

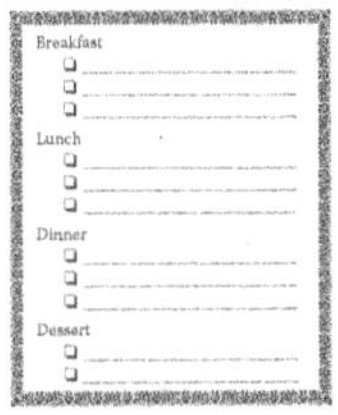

Vocabulary Skills

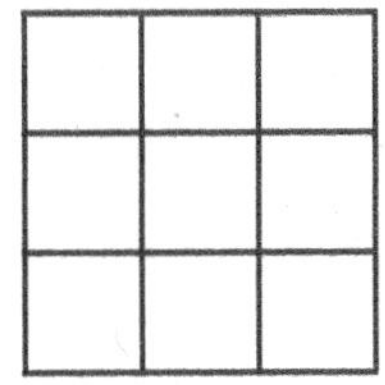

Meal Menu ▲ and Tic-Tac-Toe Menu ●

Reading Objectives Covered Through These Menus and These Activities

- Students will use resources and references to build meaning.
- Students will interpret figurative language and multiple-meaning words.

Writing Objectives Covered Through These Menus and These Activities

- Students will write to express their feelings, develop ideas, reflect, or problem solve.
- Students will exhibit voice in their writing.
- Students will use vivid language.

Materials Needed by Students for Completion

- Poster board or large white paper
- Graph paper or Internet access (for crossword puzzles)
- Blank index cards (for trading cards)
- Paper bags (for puppets)
- Socks (for puppets)
- Microsoft PowerPoint or other slideshow software ▲
- Materials for quiz boards (e.g., batteries, holiday lights, aluminum foil, tape) ●
- Materials for board games (e.g., folders, colored cards) ▲
- Materials for class games

Special Notes on the Use of These Menus

This topic has two different menu formats: Meal menu and Tic-Tac-Toe menu. The Meal menu is specifically selected for its meal-oriented, Bloom's-based options, as it is easily broken into manageable bits. The menu can be cut into strips, each strip featuring its own meal, to be given to students. This way, once students have chosen and submitted the breakfast product for grading, they can move on to the lunch strip, and lastly, they can complete the dinner and dessert strips. Because this type of menu is designed to become more advanced as students move through the meals, teachers may choose to provide their students who have special needs with just the meals and save the dessert for enrichment.

These menus give students the opportunity to create a class game. The length of the game is not stated in the product guidelines, so the teacher can determine what works best. It may be a good idea to have students start with shorter games and work up to longer games with a review focus.

The circle menu offers students the opportunity to create a quiz board. Quiz boards can range from simple to very complex, depending on the knowledge and ability of the student. Quiz boards work best when the teacher creates a "tester" that can be used to check any boards that are submitted. Basic instructions on how to create quiz boards and testers can be found at http://www.cesiscience.org/attachments/article/100/QuizBoardDirections.pdf.

Time Frame

- 2–3 weeks—Students are given the menus as the unit is started. As the teacher presents lessons throughout the week, he or she should refer back to the menu options associated with that content. The teacher will go over all of the options for that content and have students place check marks in the boxes that represent the activities they are most interested in completing. If students are using the Tic-Tac-Toe menu form, activities chosen and completed should make a column or row. If students are using the Meal menu form, students will complete one product from each meal, with dessert being an optional enrichment product. When students complete these patterns, they will have completed one activity from each content area, learning style, or level of Bloom's Revised taxonomy.
- 1 week—At the start of the unit, the teacher chooses the three activities he or she feels are most valuable for students. Stations can be set up in the classroom. These three activities are available for student choice throughout the week as regular instruction takes place.
- 1–2 days—The teacher chooses an activity from the menu to use with the entire class.

Suggested Forms

- All-purpose rubric
- Oral presentation rubric
- Student feedback rubric
- Free-choice proposal form

Name:______________________________ Date:______________ ▲

Vocabulary Skills

Directions: Choose one activity each for breakfast, lunch, and dinner. Dessert is an activity you can choose to do after you have finished your other meals. All products must be completed by: ________________.

Breakfast

- ❒ Create a set of trading cards for your vocabulary words. For each word, be sure to include a meaningful sentence that uses that word.
- ❒ Develop appropriate hand motions for all of your words to help you better understand them. Then share them with your classmates.
- ❒ Create a PowerPoint presentation that shares a picture of each vocabulary word and a meaningful sentence.

Lunch

- ❒ Using all of your vocabulary words, create a crossword puzzle. Be creative in the clues that you use. Do not always use the definition for the clue!
- ❒ Make an acrostic for at least four of your weekly words. The words you choose for each letter should be related to the word written downward.
- ❒ Design a board game to practice your vocabulary words, their definitions, and their proper use in sentences.

Dinner

- ❒ Choose at least five of your vocabulary words and write a note or letter to a person of your choice using your vocabulary words.
- ❒ Create a vocabulary puppet that helps others learn the new meanings of vocabulary words through appropriate motions and songs.
- ❒ Free choice—Submit a proposal about understanding your vocabulary words to your teacher for approval.

Dessert

- ❒ Prepare a speech that includes all of your vocabulary words. Be creative in selecting the topic of the speech and how you include the words.
- ❒ Design a class game that allows your classmates to practice their knowledge of the vocabulary words.

Name:______________________________ Date:______________

Vocabulary Skills

Directions: Check the boxes you plan to complete. They should form a tic-tac-toe across or down. All products are due by: ______________________.

☐ *Design a Greeting Card* Choose at least one of your vocabulary words and design a greeting card for a person of your choice using the sentiment expressed by that word.	☐ *Perform a Presentation* Create a vocabulary puppet that helps others learn the new meanings of vocabulary words through appropriate motions and songs.	☐ *Make an Acrostic* Make an acrostic for at least four of your weekly words. The words you choose for each letter should be related to the word written downward.
☐ *Create a Class Game* Design a class game that allows your classmates to practice their knowledge of the vocabulary words.	☐ **Free Choice: Vocabulary Skills** (Fill out your proposal form before beginning the free choice!)	☐ *Design Trading Cards* Create a set of trading cards for your vocabulary words. Be sure to include a meaningful sentence using each word.
☐ *Design a Quiz Board* Design a quiz board to practice your vocabulary words, their definitions, and their proper use in sentences.	☐ *Create a Crossword Puzzle* Using all of your vocabulary words, create a crossword puzzle. Be creative in the clues that you use. Do not always use the definition for the clue!	☐ *Prepare a Speech* Prepare a speech that includes all of your vocabulary words. Be creative in selecting the topic of the speech and how you include the words.

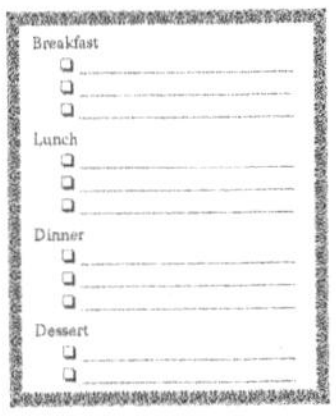

Reference Materials

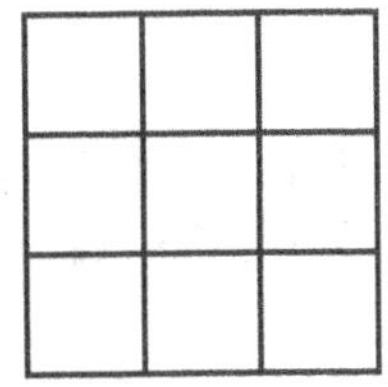

Meal Menu ▲ and Tic-Tac-Toe Menu ●

Reading Objectives Covered Through These Menus and These Activities

- Students will use resources and references to build meaning.
- Students will investigate various reference materials and their use.

Writing Objectives Covered Through These Menus and These Activities

- Students will write to express their feelings, develop ideas, reflect, or problem solve.
- Students will support their responses with textual evidence.
- Students will exhibit voice in their writing.
- Students will use vivid language.

Materials Needed by Students for Completion

- Poster board or large white paper
- Large lined index cards (for recipe cards)
- Blank index cards (for concentration cards and mobiles)
- Coat hangers (for mobiles)
- String (for mobiles)
- Internet access (for WebQuests)
- Materials for museum exhibits (e.g., boxes, cards)
- Dictionaries and thesauri

Special Notes on the Use of These Menus

This topic has two different menu formats: Meal menu and Tic-Tac-Toe menu. The Meal menu is specifically selected for its meal-oriented, Bloom's-based options, as it is easily broken into manageable bits. The menu can be cut into strips, each strip featuring its own meal, to be given to students. This way, once students have chosen and submitted the breakfast product for grading, they can move on to the lunch strip, and lastly, they can complete the dinner and dessert strips. Because this type of menu is designed to become more advanced as students move through the meals, teachers may choose to provide their students who have special needs with just the meals and save the dessert for enrichment.

These menus allow students to create a WebQuest. There are multiple versions and templates for WebQuests available on the Internet.

Teachers should decide whether to specify a certain format or allow students to create one of their own choosing.

Time Frame

- 2–3 weeks—Students are given the menus as the unit is started. As the teacher presents lessons throughout the week, he or she should refer back to the menu options associated with that content. The teacher will go over all of the options for that content and have students place check marks in the boxes that represent the activities they are most interested in completing. If students are using the Tic-Tac-Toe menu form, activities chosen and completed should make a column or row. If students are using the Meal menu form, students will complete one product from each meal, with dessert being an optional enrichment product. When students complete these patterns, they will have completed one activity from each content area, learning style, or level of Bloom's Revised taxonomy.
- 1 week—At the start of the unit, the teacher chooses the three activities he or she feels are most valuable for students. Stations can be set up in the classroom. These three activities are available for student choice throughout the week as regular instruction takes place.
- 1–2 days—The teacher chooses an activity from the menu to use with the entire class.

Suggested Forms

- All-purpose rubric
- Oral presentation rubric
- Student feedback rubric
- Free-choice proposal form

Name:_______________________________ Date:_______________ ▲

Reference Materials

Directions: Choose one activity each for breakfast, lunch, and dinner. Dessert is an activity you can choose to do after you have finished your other meals. All products must be completed by: _______________.

Breakfast

- ❒ Create a recipe card for the proper use of a dictionary to find words. Be creative!
- ❒ Design an advertisement for a dictionary. Your advertisement should convince people your age to want to use one.
- ❒ Create a concentration card game in which players match dictionary words with the guide words they might see on the top of each dictionary page. Make the game challenging!

Lunch

- ❒ The thesaurus is an effective resource for finding expressive language. Using the thesaurus, create a mobile with "great," "nice," and "said" as the top words. Under each, provide at least three other specific words with an explanation for each word.
- ❒ Using a thesaurus, write a poem that describes your personality and outlook on life.
- ❒ Design a creative book cover for a thesaurus. In your editorial comments, include examples of its use and why a student should use a thesaurus.

Dinner

- ❒ Design a museum exhibit that shows the importance of reference materials, including dictionaries and thesauri, and their use.
- ❒ Write and perform a play about a debate between a dictionary and a thesaurus. Each feels that it is most useful to students your age. This debate should settle the issue!
- ❒ Free choice—Submit a proposal about the different resources we use while writing to your teacher for approval.

Dessert

- ❒ Dictionaries have gone high tech! Create a WebQuest that takes questors through various dictionary websites, allowing them to explore and evaluate them.
- ❒ Create a children's book about an abandoned dictionary and its quest to find a teenager who will appreciate it.

Name:____ Date:____________________

Reference Materials

Directions: Check the boxes you plan to complete. They should form a tic-tac-toe across or down. All products are due by: ____________________________.

☐ *Using a Dictionary*	☐ *Writing Resources*	☐ *Using a Thesaurus*
Dictionaries have gone high tech! Create a WebQuest that takes questors through various dictionary websites, allowing them to explore and evaluate them.	Write and perform a play about a debate between a dictionary and a thesaurus. Each feels that it is most useful to students your age. This debate should settle the issue!	Design an advertisement for a thesaurus. Your advertisement should convince people your age to want to use one.
☐ *Using a Thesaurus* The thesaurus is an effective resource for finding expressive language. Using the thesaurus, create a mobile with "great," "happy," and "big" as the top words. Under each, provide at least five other specific words with an explanation for each word.	☐ **Free Choice: Using a Dictionary** (Fill out your proposal form before beginning the free choice!)	☐ *Writing Resources* Create a children's book about an abandoned dictionary and its quest to find a teenager who will appreciate it.
☐ *Writing Resources* Design a museum exhibit that shows the importance of reference materials including dictionaries and thesauri and their use.	☐ *Using a Thesaurus* Using a thesaurus, write a poem that describes your personality and outlook on life.	☐ *Using a Dictionary* Create a recipe card for the proper use of a dictionary to find words. Be creative!

Research Skills

Game Show Menus

Reading Objectives Covered Through These Menus and These Activities

- Students will compare one literary work with another.
- Students will use resources and references to build meaning.

Writing and Research Objectives Covered Through These Menus and These Activities

- Students will select well-defined research questions and frame questions to direct their own research.
- Students will communicate multiple ways to organize prior knowledge about a topic.
- Students will take notes from various sources.
- Students will summarize and organize ideas gained from multiple sources.
- Students will choose the best way to present researched information.
- Students will support their responses with textual evidence.

Materials Needed by Students for Completion

- Poster board or large white paper
- Coat hangers (for mobiles)
- Blank index cards (for mobiles and trading cards)
- String (for mobiles)
- Materials for bulletin board displays
- Large lined index cards (for instruction cards)
- Product cube template
- Materials for board games (e.g., folders, colored cards)
- DVD or VHS recorder (for videos) ●
- Internet access (for WebQuests)

Special Notes on the Use of These Menus

These menus allow students to create a bulletin board display. Some classrooms may only have one bulletin board, so the teacher can divide the board into sections, or additional classroom wall or hall space can be sectioned off for the creation of these displays. Students can plan their displays based on the amount of space they are assigned.

The circle menu gives students the opportunity to create a video. Although students enjoy producing their own videos, there are often difficulties obtaining the equipment and scheduling the use of the video recorder. The menu can be modified by allowing students to act out their videos (like a play), or if students have the technology, they may wish to produce a webcam or Flash version of their products.

Time Frame

- 2–3 weeks—Students are given the menus as the unit is started, and the guidelines and point expectations are discussed. As lessons are taught throughout the unit, students and the teacher can refer back to the options associated with the topic. The teacher will go over all of the options for the topic being covered and will have students place check marks in the boxes next to the activities they are most interested in completing. As teaching continues throughout the 2–3 weeks, activities are discussed, chosen, and submitted for grading.
- 1 week—At the beginning of the unit, the teacher chooses an activity from each area that he or she feels would be most valuable for students. Stations can be set up in the classroom. These activities are available for student choice throughout the week as regular instruction takes place.
- 1–2 days—The teacher chooses an activity from an objective to use with the entire class during lesson time.

Suggested Forms

- All-purpose rubric
- Oral presentation rubric
- Student feedback rubric
- Student-taught lesson rubric
- Point-based free-choice proposal form

Name:____ Date:____________________

Guidelines for the Research Skills Game Show Menu

- You must choose at least one activity from each topic area.
- You may not do more than two activities in any one topic area for credit. (You are, of course, welcome to do more than two for your own investigation.)
- Grading will be ongoing, so turn in products as you complete them.
- All free-choice proposals must be turned in and approved prior to working on that free-choice product.
- You must earn 120 points for a 100%. You may earn extra credit up to _____ points.
- You must show your teacher your plan for completion by: _________.

Name:____________________ Date:____________________

Research Skills

Framing Questions	Prior Knowledge	Choosing Sources	Taking Notes	Summarizing and Presenting Information	Points for Each Level
❒ Design a poster that lists five different topics your classmates may want to investigate and at least three different questions for each topic. (15 pts.)	❒ Create a mobile that shows the different ways students may choose to organize what they already know about a topic. (10 pts.)	❒ Make a windowpane that shows different types of sources you can use for research. (10 pts.)	❒ Create trading cards for three different methods that you can use to take notes. Include an example of each. (15 pts.)	❒ Make a research cube that shares six different ways you could show information you have gained through research. (15 pts.)	**10–15 points**
❒ Create Three Facts and a Fib about how to design questions for research. (20 pts.)	❒ Choose a topic you may want to research in the future. Create a mind map that shows what you already know about the topic. (25 pts.)	❒ Create an acrostic for the word "research," writing a reliable and well-chosen source that students could use for research for each letter. (20 pts.)	❒ Create an instruction card for taking notes from online sources. (20 pts.)	❒ Create a board game that allows players to go through all of the steps of the research process, from identifying a question to presenting their information. (25 pts.)	**20–25 points**
❒ Create a folded quiz book that quizzes users on their knowledge of well-written research questions. (30 pts.)	❒ Create a brochure that explains why prior knowledge is important when you research. Include some questions people can ask themselves to trigger prior knowledge. (30 pts.)	❒ Consider the following statement: "A research paper is only as good as its sources." Design a bulletin board display centered on this statement. (30 pts.)	❒ Write a flipbook that explains how to take notes from different types of sources. Place each type on one of the flaps of the book. Include examples for each source. (30 pts.)	❒ Design a WebQuest that takes questors through at least three websites that show different ways to present your researched information. Be sure to have questors evaluate the different options for presenting the information. (30 pts.)	**30 points**
Free Choice (prior approval) (25–50 pts.)	**Free Choice** (prior approval) (25–50 pts.)	**Free Choice** (prior approval) (25–50 pts.)	**Free Choice** (prior approval) (25–50 pts.)	**Free Choice** (prior approval) (25–50 pts.)	**25–50 points**
Total:	**Total:**	**Total:**	**Total:**	**Total:**	**Total Grade:**

Name:______________________ Date:______________________

Research Skills

Framing Questions	Prior Knowledge	Choosing Sources	Taking Notes	Summarizing and Presenting Information	Points for Each Level
❒ Design a poster that lists five different topics your classmates may want to investigate and at least three different questions for each topic. (10 pts.)	❒ Create a mobile that shows the different ways students may choose to organize what they already know about a topic. (10 pts.)	❒ Create an acrostic for the word "research," writing a reliable and well-chosen source that students could use for research for each letter. (15 pts.)	❒ Create an instruction card for taking notes from online sources. (10 pts.)	❒ Make a research cube that shares six different ways you could share information you have gained through research. (15 pts.)	**10–15 points**
❒ Create a folded quiz book that quizzes users on their knowledge of well-written research questions. (20 pts.)	❒ Choose a topic you may want to research in the future. Create a mind map that shows how you will organize your thoughts about the topic. (20 pts.)	❒ Consider the following statement: "A research paper is only as good as its sources." Design a bulletin board display centered on this statement. (25 pts.)	❒ Write a flipbook that explains how to take notes from different types of sources. Place each type on one of the flaps of the book. Include examples for each source. (25 pts.)	❒ Create a board game that allows players to go through all of the steps of the research process, from identifying a question to presenting their information. (25 pts.)	**20–25 points**
❒ Choose a topic you are studying in another class. Create a children's book that shares well-written research questions about this topic. Include some prior knowledge about the topic as well. (30 pts.)	❒ Before you start your journey, you must know where you are and where you want to go. Make a video that explains how this statement relates to prior knowledge when conducting research. (30 pts.)	❒ Write and perform a play about someone who does not choose the most reliable sources before a speech. (30 pts.)	❒ Create a class lesson that teaches your classmates how to take notes from different sources. (30 pts.)	❒ Design a WebQuest that takes questors through at least five websites that show different ways to present your researched information. Be sure to have questors evaluate the different options for presenting the information. (30 pts.)	**30 points**
Free Choice (prior approval) (25–50 pts.)	**Free Choice** (prior approval) (25–50 pts.)	**Free Choice** (prior approval) (25–50 pts.)	**Free Choice** (prior approval) (25–50 pts.)	**Free Choice** (prior approval) (25–50 pts.)	**25–50 points**
Total:	**Total:**	**Total:**	**Total:**	**Total:**	**Total Grade:**

Research Skills Cube

Use this template to identify six different ways you could share information you have gained through research. Provide an example of each method and how to access that method.

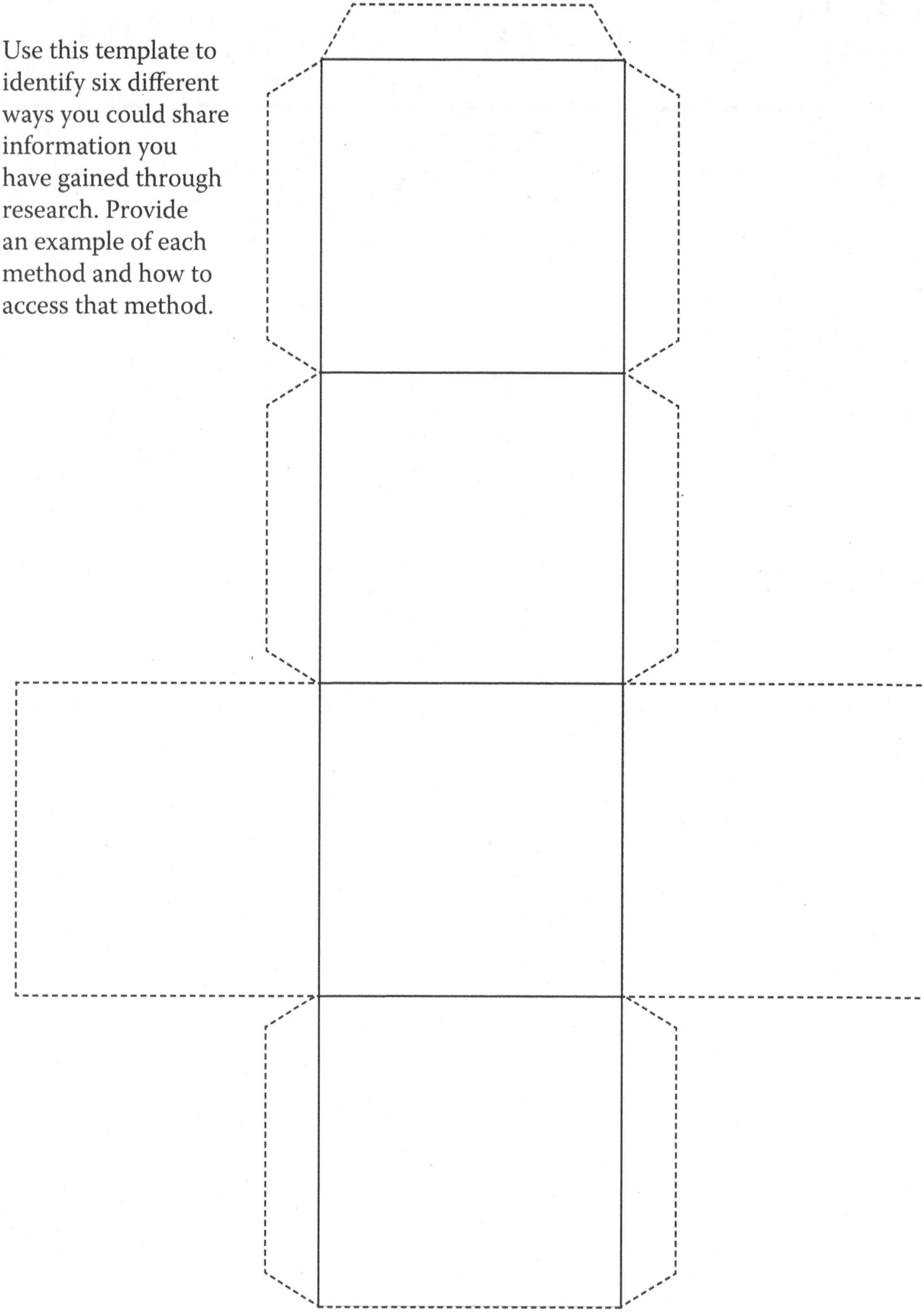

Self-Editing and Peer Editing

List Menus

Reading Objectives Covered Through These Menus and These Activities

- Students will read, analyze, and critique their own writing and that of their peers.

Writing Objectives Covered Through These Menus and These Activities

- Students will support their responses with textual evidence.
- Students will provide constructive criticism and suggestions for improvements to their writing.
- Students will revise drafts.

Materials Needed by Students for Completion

- Colored pencils (preferably not red) for editing suggestions

Time Frame

- 1–2 days—Students are given these menus in order to facilitate self- and peer editing. The menus can be given before the writing process begins so that students will know what others will be looking for when editing, or they can receive the menus after they've already written their first drafts. The students choose from among the available options to edit their and classmates' papers in various ways.

Suggested Forms

- All-purpose rubric
- Point-based free-choice proposal form

Name:_______________________________________ Date:_______________________

Self-Editing and Peer Editing

Guidelines:

1. You may complete as many of the activities listed as you can within the time period.
2. You may choose any combination of activities.
3. Your goal is 50 points. You may earn up to _____ points extra credit.
4. You may be as creative as you like within the guidelines listed below.
5. You must show your plan to your teacher by _________________.
6. Activities may be turned in at any time during the working time period. They will be graded and recorded on this sheet as you continue to work, so keep it safe!

Plan to Do	Activity to Complete (5–20 Points)	Point Value	Date Completed	Points Earned
	Check the paper for proper spelling and capitalization.	5		
	Check commas and quotation marks to be sure they are used properly.	5		
	Check the paper to be sure all of the sentences are complete, with no fragments or run-ons.	10		
	Check for overused words (any nouns or verbs that are used more than three times) and circle them.	10		
	As you read, write at least two questions about what you are reading that could help improve the writing. Write your questions next to the paragraphs to which they relate.	15		
	Check for slang or "teen" words and put a square around them. Make a suggestion for a better word.	15		
	Check the assignment for any off-topic sentences or information. Mark the information and note why it seems to be off topic.	15		
	Locate and mark at least one sentence that could be made better by adding additional details and suggest some details that could be used.	15		
	Free choice—Prepare a proposal form and submit your idea for approval.	5–15		
	Look at all of the vocabulary used in the assignment and suggest at least three specific words that could replace weaker words currently being used.	20		
	Comment on what you think is the best part of the assignment. Your comment should be specific and constructive.	20		
	Read the paper backwards, from the end to the beginning, one sentence at a time, to double check for grammatical errors. Make at least two suggestions for improving the paper.	20		
	Total number of points you are planning to earn.	**Total points earned:**		

I am planning to complete ____ activities that could earn up to a total of _____ points.

Teacher's initials _______ Student's signature ______________________________

Name:______________________________ Date:______________________

Self-Editing and Peer Editing

Guidelines:

1. You may complete as many of the activities listed as you can within the time period.
2. You may choose any combination of activities.
3. Your goal is 50 points. You may earn up to _____ points extra credit.
4. You may be as creative as you like within the guidelines listed below.
5. You must show your plan to your teacher by ________________.
6. Activities may be turned in at any time during the working time period. They will be graded and recorded on this sheet as you continue to work, so keep it safe!

Plan to Do	Activity to Complete (5–20 Points)	Point Value	Date Completed	Points Earned
	Check the paper for proper spelling and capitalization.	5		
	Check commas and quotation marks to be sure they are used properly.	5		
	As you read, write at least two more questions about what you are reading that could help improve the writing. Write your questions next to the paragraphs to which they relate.	10		
	Check for slang or "teen" words and put a square around them. Make a suggestion for a better word.	10		
	Check the paper to be sure all of the sentences are complete, with no fragments or run-ons.	10		
	Locate and mark at least one sentence that could be made better by adding additional details and suggest some details that could be used.	10		
	Look at all of the vocabulary used in the assignment and suggest at least three specific words that could replace weaker words currently being used.	15		
	Check the assignment for proper paragraph structure. Does it follow the assigned structure? If so, provide a positive comment about the structure. If not, provide a constructive comment to help improve the structure.	15		
	Comment on what you think is the best part of the assignment. Your comment should be specific and constructive.	15		
	If appropriate, locate and comment on the use of voice in the writing. If voice is not present, but could be, provide constructive ideas on how to integrate it.	15		
	Read the paper backwards, from the end to the beginning, one sentence at a time, to double check for grammatical errors. Make at least two suggestions for improving the paper.	15		
	Free choice—Prepare a proposal form and submit your idea for approval.	5–15		
	Read the assignment aloud to a classmate and ask for two specific suggestions on how to make it better.	20		
	Total number of points you are planning to earn.		**Total points earned:**	

I am planning to complete ____ activities that could earn up to a total of _____ points.

Teacher's initials _______ Student's signature _________________________

Author's Purpose

Meal Menu ▲ and Tic-Tac-Toe Menu ●

Reading Objectives Covered Through These Menus and These Activities

- Students will distinguish between an author's opinion and fact.
- Students will investigate works written to persuade, inform, and entertain.
- Students will be able to identify characteristics of each type of writing.

Writing Objectives Covered Through These Menus and These Activities

- Students will write to express their feelings, develop ideas, reflect, or problem solve.
- Students will exhibit voice in their writing.

Materials Needed by Students for Completion

- Microsoft PowerPoint or other slideshow software
- Paper bags (for puppets)
- Socks (for puppets)
- Large lined index cards (for recipe cards) ●
- DVD or VHS recorder (for news reports)

Special Notes on the Use of These Menus

This topic has two different menu formats: Meal menu and Tic-Tac-Toe menu. The Meal menu is specifically selected for its meal-oriented, Bloom's-based options, as it is easily broken into manageable bits. The menu can be cut into strips, each strip featuring its own meal, to be given to students. This way, once students have chosen and submitted the breakfast product for grading, they can move on to the lunch strip, and lastly, they can complete the dinner and dessert strips. Because this type of menu is designed to become more advanced as students move through the meals, teachers may choose to provide their students who have special needs with just the meals and save the dessert for enrichment.

These menus give students the opportunity to create a news report. Although students enjoy producing their own videos, there are often difficulties obtaining the equipment and scheduling the use of the video recorder. The menus can be modified by allowing students to act out their news reports (like a play), or if students have the technology, they may wish to produce a webcam or Flash version of their news reports.

Time Frame

- 2–3 weeks—Students are given the menus as the unit is started. As the teacher presents lessons throughout the week, he or she should refer back to the menu options associated with that content. The teacher will go over all of the options for that content and have students place check marks in the boxes that represent the activities they are most interested in completing. If students are using the Tic-Tac-Toe menu form, activities chosen and completed should make a column or row. If students are using the Meal menu form, students will complete one product from each meal, with dessert being an optional enrichment product. When students complete these patterns, they will have completed one activity from each content area, learning style, or level of Bloom's Revised taxonomy.
- 1 week—At the start of the unit, the teacher chooses the three activities he or she feels are most valuable for students. Stations can be set up in the classroom. These three activities are available for student choice throughout the week as regular instruction takes place.
- 1–2 days—The teacher chooses an activity from the menu to use with the entire class.

Suggested Forms

- All-purpose rubric
- Oral presentation rubric
- Student feedback rubric
- Free-choice proposal form

Name:____ Date:______________________

Author's Purpose

Directions: Choose one activity each for breakfast, lunch, and dinner. Dessert is an activity you can choose to do after you have finished your other meals. All products must be completed by: ____________________.

Breakfast

- ❒ Create a poster that shares various examples of books and short stories that were written specifically to entertain.
- ❒ Write a letter to a friend or family member describing something fun you have done this month. Be descriptive so the person feels like he or she was there with you.
- ❒ Free choice—Submit a proposal in which you write to entertain to your teacher for approval.

Lunch

- ❒ Write an informative children's book about your community.
- ❒ Select a career that interests you and interview at least two people who work in that area. Create a brochure that shares the information you obtained.
- ❒ Create a news report that shares important information about what is happening at your school.

Dinner

- ❒ Parents are lobbying the state to change the age at which someone can get a driver's license—to age 21! Research possible reasons for this idea. Write and perform a persuasive speech that shares your thoughts on this movement.
- ❒ Create a persuasion puppet that is always trying to make others do what it wants. Perform a persuasive puppet show with your puppet.
- ❒ Choose an issue that is impacting people your age that you feel is important. Create a persuasive PowerPoint presentation to convince others to agree with your point of view.

Dessert

- ❒ Choose an author who writes with the purpose of entertaining his or her readers. Prepare a You Be the Person presentation in which you come to class as your author and discuss your written works and how you write specifically to entertain your readers.
- ❒ Write a letter to your local newspaper about your school and upcoming events for the next month. You may need to interview some people at your school to obtain enough information. Send your letter to the newspaper once you've written it.

Name:______________________________ Date:____________________

Author's Purpose

Directions: Check the boxes you plan to complete. They should form a tic-tac-toe across or down. All products are due by: ________________________.

☐ *Entertain*	☐ *Persuade*	☐ *Inform*
Create a PowerPoint presentation that shares various examples of books and short stories that were written specifically to entertain. Your presentation should focus on the aspects of the written work that let you know it was written to entertain.	Parents are lobbying the state to change the age at which someone can get a driver's license—to age 21! Research possible reasons for this idea. Write and perform a persuasive speech that shares your thoughts on this movement.	Write a recipe card that could be used to write an informative children's book about your community. Then write the book.
☐ *Inform* Create a news report that shares important information about what is happening at your school.	☐ **Free Choice: Writing to Entertain** (Fill out your proposal form before beginning the free choice!)	☐ *Persuade* Choose an issue that is impacting people your age that you feel is important. Write a persuasive newspaper article to convince others to agree with your point of view.
☐ *Persuade* Create a persuasion puppet that is always trying to make others do what it wants. Perform a persuasive puppet show with your puppet.	☐ *Inform* Write a letter to your local newspaper about your school and upcoming events for the next month. You may need to interview some people at your school to obtain enough information. Send your letter to the newspaper once you've written it.	☐ *Entertain* Choose an author who writes with the purpose of entertaining his or her readers. Prepare a You Be the Person presentation in which you come to class as your author and discuss your written works and how you write specifically to entertain your readers.

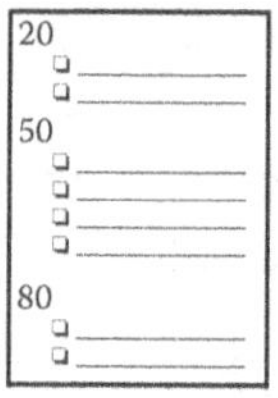

Identifying Bias

20-50-80 Menus

Reading Objectives Covered Through These Menus and These Activities

- Students will prove conclusions using textual evidence.
- Students will analyze informational texts for author bias (e.g., word choice and the exclusion and inclusion of particular information).
- Students will use resources and references to build meaning.

Writing Objectives Covered Through These Menus and These Activities

- Students will support their responses with textual evidence.
- Students will write to inform, explain, describe, or narrate.
- Students will revise drafts.

Materials Needed by Students for Completion

- Poster board or large white paper
- Large lined index cards (for instruction cards)
- Newspapers and magazines (for collages) ●
- Internet access (for articles) ▲
- Microsoft PowerPoint or other slideshow software
- DVD or VHS recorder (for news reports)
- Materials for bulletin board displays
- Materials for mobiles (e.g., coat hangers, string, cards) ▲
- Coat hangers (for mobiles) ▲
- Blank index cards (for mobiles) ▲
- String (for mobiles) ▲

Special Notes on the Use of These Menus

These menus give students the opportunity to create a news report. Although students enjoy producing their own videos, there are often difficulties obtaining the equipment and scheduling the use of the video recorder. The menus can be modified by allowing students to act out their news reports (like a play), or if students have the technology, they may wish to produce a webcam or Flash version of their news reports.

These menus also allows students to create a bulletin board display. Some classrooms may only have one bulletin board, so the teacher can divide the board into sections, or additional classroom wall or hall space can be sectioned off for the creation of these displays. Students can plan their displays based on the amount of space they are assigned.

Time Frame

- 1–2 weeks—Students are given the menus as the unit is started, and the teacher discusses all of the product options on the menus. As the different options are discussed, students will choose products that add to a total of 100 points. As the lessons progress, the teacher and students refer back to the menu options associated with the content being taught.
- 1–2 days—The teacher chooses an activity or product from the menu to use with the entire class.

Suggested Forms

- All-purpose rubric
- Oral presentation rubric
- Student feedback rubrics
- Point-based free-choice proposal form

Name:______________________________________ Date:__________________

Identifying Bias

Directions: Choose at least two activities from the menu below. The activities must total at least 100 points. Place a check mark next to each box to show which activities you will complete. All activities must be completed by: ____________________.

20 Points

- ❒ Select two Internet articles about the same event, one that shows bias and one that does not. Highlight the statements in the article that show bias.
- ❒ Create a mobile of words, pictures, and short articles that show examples of bias.

50 Points

- ❒ Create a poster that shows examples of bias in both writing and the media.
- ❒ Find a comic strip that shows bias. Make a bulletin board display for the comic strip showing why it is biased and how it could be rewritten to be free of bias.
- ❒ Design an instruction card that details how to write without bias.
- ❒ Design a brochure that explains and provides examples of bias in writing and the media. Include how to recognize bias and why authors and reporters may choose to use bias.

80 Points

- ❒ Contact a local newspaper or television reporter and interview that person about bias in his or her job. Using his or her responses, create your own news report about how bias impacts us in our daily lives.
- ❒ Even authors with the best intentions have difficulty being completely unbiased in their written works. Analyze the reading selection you are working with in order to determine the author's bias. Prepare a PowerPoint presentation in which you share your knowledge of bias and quotes found in your reading selection that show the author's bias.

Name:____ Date:____________________

Identifying Bias

Directions: Choose at least two activities from the menu below. The activities must total at least 100 points. Place a check mark next to each box to show which activities you will complete. All activities must be completed by: _______________________.

20 Points

- ❐ Create a collage of words, pictures, and short articles that show examples of bias.
- ❐ Create a folded quiz book that has users determine examples of bias in both writing and the media.

50 Points

- ❐ Design a brochure that explains and provides examples of bias in writing and the media. Include how to recognize bias and why authors and reporters may choose to use bias.
- ❐ Design an instruction card that details how to write without bias.
- ❐ Find a comic strip that shows bias. Make a poster for the comic strip explaining why it is biased and how it could be written so it is free of bias.
- ❐ Contact a local newspaper or television reporter and interview that person about bias in his or her job. Using his or her responses, create your own news report about how bias impacts us in our daily lives.

80 Points

- ❐ Create a bulletin board display that shows the different types of bias a reader could encounter. Include quotes from a current reading selection as examples of biased and nonbiased writing.
- ❐ Even authors with the best intentions have difficulty being completely unbiased in their written works. Analyze the reading selection you are working with in order to determine the author's bias. Prepare a PowerPoint presentation in which you share your knowledge of bias and quotes found in your reading selection that show your author's bias.

Resources

Note: These resources have been specifically chosen to address a wide range of ability levels. All of the books have a grades 6–8 interest level, but the reading levels vary.

Biography

Adler, D. A. (2001). *B. Franklin, printer.* New York, NY: Holiday House.

Aliki. (2000). *William Shakespeare & the Globe.* New York, NY: HarperCollins.

Alter, J. (2000). *Extraordinary explorers and adventurers.* New York, NY: Children's Press.

Berenstain, S., & Berenstain, J. (2002). *Down a sunny dirt road: An autobiography.* New York, NY: Random House.

Bragg, R. (1998). *All over but the shoutin'.* New York, NY: Vintage.

Brooks, T. (2004). *Sometimes the magic works: Lessons from a writing life.* New York, NY: Del Rey.

Danneberg, J. (2002). *Women artists of the west: Five portraits in creativity and courage.* Golden, CO: Fulcrum.

Flowers, P., & Dixon, A. (2003). *Alone across the Arctic: One woman's epic journey by dog team.* Portland, OR: Alaska Northwest Books.
Gantos, J. (2004). *Hole in my life.* New York, NY: Farrar, Strauss and Giroux.
Jacobsen, R. (2001). *Rescued images: Memories of a childhood in hiding.* New York, NY: Mikaya Press.
Macy, S. (2006). *Bull's eye: A photobiography of Annie Oakley.* Washington, DC: National Geographic Society.
Stanley, D. (2000). *Leonardo da Vinci.* New York, NY: HarperCollins.
Zoya (with Follain, J., & Cristofari, R.). (2003). *Zoya's story: An Afghan woman's struggle for freedom.* New York, NY: HarperCollins.

Drama

Fleischman, P. (2001). *Mind's eye.* New York, NY: Laurel-Leaf.
Gallo, D. R. (Ed.). (1991). *Center stage: One-act plays for teenage readers and actors.* New York, NY: HarperCollins.
Kehret, P. (1991). *Acting natural: Monologues, dialogs, and playlets for teens.* Colorado Springs, CO: Meriwether.
Lamb, W. (Ed.). (1987). *Ground zero club.* New York, NY: Laurel-Leaf.
Mecca, J. T. (1997). *Real-life drama for real, live students: A collection of monologues, duet acting, scenes, & a full-length play.* Nashville, TN: Incentive.
Slaight, C., & Sharrar, J. (Eds.). (1996). *Short plays for young actors.* Newbury, VT: Smith & Kraus.
Smith, R., & Avi. (1997). *Nothing but the truth: A play.* New York, NY: Avon.
Soto, G. (1999). *Nerdlandia.* New York, NY: Putnam.

Graphic Novels

Argones, S. (2002). *The Groo maiden.* Milwaukie, OR: Dark Horse Comics.
Briggs, R. (2001). *Ethel and Ernest: A true story.* New York, NY: Pantheon Books.
Cooper, G. (2007). *The Trojan horse.* Milwaukee, WI: World Almanac Library.
Eisner, W. (2006). *A contract with God.* New York, NY: W. W. Norton.

Eisner, W., Russell, P. C., McCrae, J., Powell, E., Muth, J. J., Chelsea, D. ... Gibbons, D. (2002). *9-11: Artists respond, volume 1.* Milwaukie, OR: Dark Horse Comics.

Gonick, L. (1997). *Cartoon history of the universe.* New York, NY: Main Street Books.

Heuet, S., & Proust, M. (2003). *Remembrance of things past: Combray.* New York, NY: NBM.

Higson, C., & Walker, K. (2010). *Young Bond: SilverFin: The graphic novel.* New York, NY: Disney/Hyperion Books.

Johnston, A. (2009). *Skeleton key.* New York, NY: Philomel.

Kiyama, H. (1999). *The four immigrants manga: A Japanese experience in San Francisco, 1904–1924.* Berkeley, CA: Stone Bridge Press.

Marz, R. (2002). *Sojourn: From the ashes.* Oldsmar, FL: CrossGeneration.

Miller, F., & Varley, L. (1999). *300.* Milwaukie, OR: Dark Horse Comics.

Moore, S., & Jacques, B. (2007). *Redwall: The graphic novel.* New York, NY: Philomel Books.

Ottaviani, J. (2003). *Dignifying science: Stories about women scientists* (2nd ed.). Ann Arbor, MI: G. T. Labs.

Peters, S. T. (2009). *Rapunzel: The graphic novel.* Minneapolis, MN: Stone Arch Books.

Tanaka, M. (2011). *Gon 1.* New York, NY: Kodansha Comics.

Toriyama, A. (2000). *Dragonball Z.* San Francisco, CA: Viz Media LLC.

Waid, M., McCraw, T., & Peyer, T. (1999). *Legion of super-heroes: The beginning of tomorrow.* New York, NY: DC Comics.

Yang, G. L. (2008). *American born Chinese.* New York, NY: Square Fish.

Mystery and Suspense

Beil, M. (2011). *The Red Blazer Girls: The vanishing violin.* New York, NY: Knopf.

Bosch, P. (2009). *If you're reading this, it's too late.* New York, NY: Little Brown.

Brezenoff, S. (2009). *The painting that wasn't there.* Minneapolis, MN: Stone Arch Books.

Brezenoff, S. (2009). *The teacher who forgot too much.* Minneapolis, MN: Stone Arch Books.

Broach, E. (2010). *Masterpiece.* New York, NY: Holt/Christy Ottaviano Books.

Chatterton, M. (2009). *The Brain finds a leg.* Atlanta, GA: Peachtree.

Dowd, S. (2009). *The London Eye mystery.* New York, NY: Yearling.
Feinstein, J. (2009). *Change-up: Mystery at the World Series.* New York, NY: Alfred A. Knopf.
Feinstein, J. (2010). *The rivalry: Mystery at the Army-Navy game.* New York, NY: Knopf.
Flavin, T. (2012). *The Blackhope enigma.* Somerville, MA: Candlewick Press.
Hahn, M. D. (2010). *Closed for the season: A mystery story.* Boston, MA: Clarion Books.
Haines, K. M. (2012). *The girl is murder.* New York, NY: Roaring Brook Press.
Harrison, M. (2011). *13 treasures.* New York, NY: Little Brown.
Hunter, E. (2009). *The fourth apprentice.* New York, NY: Harper.
Lasky, K. (2010). *Lone wolf.* New York, NY: Scholastic Press.
Markle, S. (2011). *The case of the vanishing golden frogs: A scientific mystery.* Minneapolis, MN: Milbrook Press.
Morton-Shaw, C. (2009). *The hunt for the seventh.* New York, NY: Katherine Tegen Books.
Newsome, R. (2010). *The billionaire's curse.* New York, NY: Walden Pond Press.
O'Neill, T. (2007). *Chupacabra.* Detroit, MI: KidHaven Press.
Peacock, S. (2009). *Vanishing girl.* Toronto, Ontario: Tundra Books.
Scott, E., & O'Brien, J. (2008). *All about sleep from a to zzzz.* New York, NY: Viking.
Sensel, J. (2010). *The Farwalker's quest.* New York, NY: Bloomsbury.
Smith, R. (2009). *Tentacles.* New York, NY: Scholastic Press.
Stead, R. (2010). *When you reach me.* New York, NY: Yearling.
Weatherly, L. (2011). *Angel burn.* Somerville, MA: Candlewick Press.

Poetry

Adoff, A. (1995). *Slow dance heartbreak blues.* New York, NY: HarperCollins.
Appelt, K. (2010). *Poems from homeroom: A writer's place to start.* New York, NY: Owlet Paperbacks.
Carlson, L. M. (1995). *Cool salsa: Bilingual poems on growing up Latino in the United States.* New York, NY: Fawcett Juniper.
Corrigan, E. (2002). *You remind me of you: A poetry memoir.* New York, NY: Push.

Fleischman P. (2004). *Joyful noise: Poems for two voices.* New York, NY: HarperCollins.

Gilroy, T., Grace, A., McKay, J., Martin, D. A., Phillips, G. L., & Roth, R. (2004). *The Haiku year* (2nd ed.). Brooklyn, NY: Soft Skull Press.

Glenn, M. (1999). *Who killed Mr. Chippendale? A mystery in poems.* New York, NY: Puffin.

Gordon, R. (1995). *Pierced by a ray of sun: Poems about the times we feel alone.* New York, NY: HarperCollins.

Hughes, L. (2007). *The dream keeper and other poems.* New York, NY: Knopf Books for Young Readers. (Original work published 1932)

Janeczko, P. B. (2000). *Stone bench in an empty park.* New York, NY: Scholastic.

Kherdian, D. (1996). *Beat voices: An anthology of beat poetry.* New York, NY: HarperCollins.

Lawson, J. (2008). *Black stars in a white night sky.* Honesdale, PA: Wordsong.

Nye, N. S. (2001). *What have you lost?* New York, NY: HarperTeen.

Silverstein, S. (1964). *A giraffe and a half.* New York, NY: HarperCollins.

Silverstein, S. (1981). *A light in the attic.* New York, NY: HarperCollins.

Silverstein, S. (1996). *Falling up.* New York, NY: HarperCollins.

Silverstein, S. (2011). *Every thing on it.* New York, NY: HarperCollins.

Vecchione, P. (2007). *Faith & doubt: An anthology of poems.* New York, NY: Henry Holt.

Von Ziegesar, C. (Ed.). (2000). *Slam.* New York, NY: Puffin Books.

Science Fiction

Adams, D. (2004). *The hitchhiker's guide to the galaxy.* New York, NY: Harmony Books. (Original work published 1979)

Allen, R. M. (2001). *The depths of time.* New York, NY: Bantam.

Anderson, M. T. (2012). *Feed.* Cambridge, MA: Candlewick.

Bennett, C., & Gottesfeld, J. (2002). *Anne Frank and me.* New York, NY: Putnam.

Butler, O. E. (2000). *Parable of the talents.* New York, NY: Seven Stories Press.

Collins, S. (2008). *The hunger games.* New York, NY: Scholastic Press.

Collins, S. (2009). *Catching fire.* New York, NY: Scholastic Press.

Collins, S. (2010). *Mockingjay.* New York, NY: Scholastic Press.

Dashner, J. (2009). *The journal of curious letters.* New York, NY: Aladdin.

Haldeman, J. (1998). *Forever peace.* New York, NY: Ace.
Hughes, M. P. (2011). *A crack in the sky.* New York, NY: Yearling.
Kress, N. (2004). *Crossfire.* New York, NY: Tor.
L'Engle, M. (2012). *A wrinkle in time: 50th anniversary commemorative edition.* New York, NY: Farrar, Strauss and Giroux.
Lowry, L. (2006). *The giver.* New York, NY: Ember.
Lowry, L. (2009). *Messenger.* New York, NY: Bantam.
Lowry, L. (2012). *Gathering blue.* Boston, MA: Houghton Mifflin Books for Children.
Paulsen, G. (2002). *The white fox chronicles.* New York, NY: Laurel Leaf.
Pfeffer, S. B. (2008). *Life as we knew it.* Orlando, FL: Harcourt.
Roberts, J. M. (2003). *Hannibal's children.* New York, NY: Ace.
Schanback, M. (2005). *Princess from another planet.* New York, NY: Holiday House.
Shusterman, N. (2003). *Shattered sky.* New York, NY: Tor.
Vande Velde, V. (2004). *Heir apparent.* Orlando, FL: Harcourt.
Vizzini, N. (2005). *Be more chill.* New York, NY: Miramax.
Weaver, W. (2012). *Memory boy.* New York, NY: HarperTeen.
Westerfeld, S. (2011). *Uglies.* New York, NY: Simon Pulse.

References

Anderson, L., & Krathwohl, D. (Eds.). (2001). *A taxonomy for learning, teaching, and assessing: A revision of Bloom's taxonomy for educational objectives* (Complete ed.). New York, NY: Longman.

Magner, L. (2000). Reaching all children through differentiated assessment: The 2-5-8 plan. *Gifted Child Today, 23*(3), 48–50.

Mercer, C. D., Lane, H. B., Jordan, L., Allsopp, D. H., & Eisele, M. R. (1996). Empowering teachers and students with instructional choices in inclusive settings. *Remedial & Special Education, 17,* 226–236.

About the Author

After teaching science for more than 15 years, both overseas and in the U.S., **Laurie E. Westphal** now works as an independent gifted education and science consultant nationwide. She enjoys developing and presenting staff development on differentiation for various districts and conferences, working with teachers to assist them in planning and developing lessons to meet the needs of all students. Laurie currently resides in Houston, TX, and has made it her goal to convert as many teachers as she can to the differentiated lifestyle in the classroom and share her vision for real-world, product-based lessons that help all students become critical thinkers and effective problem solvers.

If you are interested in having Laurie speak at your next staff development day or conference, please visit her website, http://www.giftedconsultant.com, for additional information.

Common Core State Standards Alignment

This book aligns with an extensive number of the Common Core State Standards for ELA-Literacy. Please visit http://www.Taylor & Francis.com/ccss to download a complete packet of the standards that align with each individual menu in this book.

Additional Titles by the Author

Laurie E. Westphal has written many books on using differentiation strategies in the classroom, providing teachers of grades K–12 with creative, engaging, ready-to-use resources. Among them are:

Math, Language Arts, Science, and Social Studies volumes available for:

Differentiating Instruction With Menus, Grades K–2

Differentiating Instruction With Menus, Grades 3–5, Second Edition

Differentiating Instruction With Menus, Grades 6–8, Second Edition

Math, Language Arts, Science, and Social Studies volumes available for:

Differentiating Instruction With Menus for the Inclusive Classroom, Grades K–2

Differentiating Instruction With Menus for the Inclusive Classroom, Grades 3–5

Differentiating Instruction With Menus for the Inclusive Classroom, Grades 6–8

Literature for Every Learner, Grades 3–5; 6–8; and 9–12

Differentiating Instruction With Menus: Algebra I/II, Grades 9–12

Differentiating Instruction With Menus: Biology, Grades 9–12

For a current listing of Laurie's books, please visit Taylor & Francis **at http://www.**Taylor & Francis**.com.**